God's Got A Miracle For You

Dedication:

This book is dedicated to four men who helped me find the truth of Jesus Christ. Until you find truth, you will never find all that the Lord has for you. Thank you, Corey Carswell, David Bridges, Harold Davis and Chris Capulso. Each of you have brought such light and revelation into my life. I will be eternally grateful. This book is dedicated to you guys.

Preface:

Friend I want you to realize that God is still a miracle worker today and can do far more than you are seeing Him do in your life at this moment. In this book my hope and prayer is to lead you into the greater miracles of God and to help you get on the path of abundance that He has promised those who have truly become His. Jesus is the same yesterday, today and forever.

That being said we can see, looking at the story of Joshua and his being led of God into the Promised Land how we might receive the same kind of mind-blowing miracles and abundance in our life. We, just like the children of Israel at the time, live way below what God has promised for us. The children of Israel had so much more than they were receiving. My dear friend if you will follow these few simple steps as outlined in this book, I believe you are going to start seeing a shift in your life as well. Remember do not be just a reader of this word, but apply it and walk in it and see if you don't start seeing the great miracle working power of God in your life.

Chapter 1

Receiving God's Promised Miracles

Joshua 3:5-17

Joshua 3:5-17

And Joshua said unto the people, Sanctify yourselves: for to morrow the LORD will do wonders among you. And Joshua spake unto the priests, saying, Take up the ark of the covenant, and pass over before the people. And they took up the ark of the covenant, and went before the people. And the LORD said unto Joshua, This day will I begin to magnify thee in the sight of all Israel, that they may know that, as I was with Moses, so I will be with thee. And thou shalt command the priests that bear the ark of the covenant, saying, When ye are come to the brink of the water of Jordan, ye shall stand still in Jordan. And Joshua said unto the children of Israel, Come hither, and hear the words of the LORD your God. And Joshua said, Hereby ye shall know that the living God is among you, and that he will without fail drive out from before you the Canaanites, and the Hittites, and the Hivites, and the Perizzites, and the Girgashites, and the Amorites, and the Jebusites. Behold, the ark of the covenant of the LORD of all the earth passeth over before you into Jordan. Now therefore take you twelve men out of the tribes of Israel, out of every tribe a man. And it shall come to pass, as soon as the soles of the feet of the priests that bear the ark of the LORD, the LORD of all the earth, shall rest in the waters of Jordan, that the waters of Jordan shall be cut off from the waters that come down from above; and they shall stand upon an heap. And it came to pass, when the people removed from their tents, to pass over Jordan, and the priests bearing the ark of the covenant before the people; And as they that bare the ark were come unto Jordan, and the feet of the priests that bare the ark were dipped in the brim of the water, (for Jordan overfloweth all his banks all the time of harvest,) That the waters which came down from above stood and rose up upon an heap very far from the city Adam, that is beside Zaretan: and those that came down toward the sea of the plain, even the salt sea, failed, and were cut off: and the people passed over right against Jericho. And the priests that bare the ark of the covenant of the LORD stood firm on dry ground in the midst of Jordan, and all the Israelites passed over on dry ground, until all the people were passed clean over Jordan.

God wants to perform miracles in your life. He wants to part your Red Seas, tear down the walls of your enemies and take down your giants. This chapter is more of an overview of the rest of the book on receiving God's miracles. We are going to look at the seven steps to receiving Gods miracles in this chapter and then in the chapters following we will break down each step in more detail.
Do you believe in miracles?
I hope so, because it is our faith in a supernatural God that causes Christians to believe that unexplainable events outside the natural realm do occur from time to time.

Mirriam-Webster's online dictionary defines "miracle" as, "an extraordinary event manifesting divine intervention in human affairs".

Back in 2000, Newsweek took a poll concerning the topic of miracles and here are some of the results.

· 84% believe God performs miracles.

· 79% believe the miracles in the Bible actually took place.

· 63% know someone who claims to have experienced a miracle.

· 48% say they have experienced or witnessed one.

· 90% of Christians believe in miracles.

· 46% of non-Christians do.

· 98% of Evangelical Protestants believe in miracles.

· 87% agree miracles can happen to religious faiths different than their own.

· 67% of Americans have prayed for a miracle.

· 77% believe miracles can cure people given no chance by medical doctors.

Now this should be an encouragement to all of us to share our faith because we know that not every one of those who believe in miracles is born again.
But, if they believe there is a God who works miracles then they must be open to the greatest supernatural work of all – salvation.

Having served in many countries, I have found that no other religion can validate its message like the message of Jesus can.

The problem we see in America then is not with God working miracles, but with the question, "Can we expect God to work miracles on our behalf when we pray?"

And the answer is a resounding "YES!" Even though some Christians do not believe that God works miracles on our behalf, the bible is very clear on what God desires to do for those who trust Him.

Let us look at a passage from the book of Joshua and see the steps that lead to a great miracle on behalf of the nation of Israel.

1. In order to receive God's Miracles we have to be living a consecrated, sanctified life.

Joshua told the people:

Joshua 3:5
And Joshua said unto the people, Sanctify yourselves: for to morrow the Lord will do wonders among you.

The word "sanctify" means "to be made clean or holy". It is presumptuous of us to think that just because we have been saved by God's grace through our faith in Jesus that we can live our lives in any fashion we desire and expect God to respond to our prayers.

God is not our magician.

Deuteronomy 23:14
*For the Lord thy God walketh in the midst of thy camp, to deliver thee, and to give up thine enemies before thee; therefore shall thy camp be **holy**: that he see no unclean thing in thee, and turn away from thee.*

Again the Lord says

1ˢᵗ Peter 1:15-16
But as he which hath called you is holy, so be ye holy in all manner of conversation; Because it is written, Be ye holy; for I am holy.

Your camp must be holy, so that He will not see among you anything indecent and turn away from you.

Friend, the first step in becoming sanctified and holy is to repent of your sins, be baptized for the remission of your sins and receive the Holy Ghost.

We are not talking about being legalistic. We can tie our hair up in a bun or have it cut above the ears, wear long sleeved shirts or long dresses, not go to movies and be in church every time the doors are opened, but that doesn't mean our heart is right before the Lord.

Sanctification and consecration come from a personal relationship with the Risen Savior.

Sanctification and consecration come from separating yourself from the lies of the world.
Sanctification and consecration come from crucifying the flesh.

The generation before this generation of Israelites who were about to go into the land of promise, even though they had left Egypt, never really separated themselves from Egypt.

They were not sanctified, consecrated or set apart.

That is why they all died in the desert. It is hard to imagine what God must have thought as His presence was in the middle of the camp day and night, in sight of all of Israel, and all He heard from them was grumbling and complaining about the food and the conditions? Can you imagine?

They want quail – I'll give them quail… And as they stood and danced around the fire that had somehow miraculously produced a golden calf, they worshipped the calf while calling on the name of the Lord?

Even though they had been removed from the sin of Egypt, they never sanctified and consecrated themselves to God. Even though they were in the presence of God, their heart was far from God.

Once we are saved, sanctifying and consecrating ourselves means crucifying the flesh.

We do not get saved and keep on doing the same things we always did.

Ephesians 2:10
For we are his workmanship, created in Christ Jesus unto good works, which God hath before ordained that we should walk in them.

What would have happened if Israel had not sanctified and consecrated themselves to the Lord?

Would God have done amazing things among them?
Do we want to see God do great miracles in our life? If so, we have to surrender ourselves to God allowing Him to

sanctify us and consecrate us once again. It is He that has to do the cleaning, we have to be yielded.

2. <u>Joshua tells the people to go and stand in the river.</u>

Joshua 3:8
And thou shalt command the priests that bear the ark of the covenant, saying, When ye are come to the brink of the water of Jordan, ye shall stand still in Jordan.

God told Joshua, "Tell the priests who carry the Ark of the Covenant: 'When you reach the edge of the Jordan's waters, go and stand in the river.'"

There are two things about standing in the river.

1) The river was what was keeping Israel from getting into the Promised Land. The Jordan River at flood stage can be as much as one mile wide.

Do we want to see God work miracles in our life? Then we have to confront the obstruction head on.

Are you having a hard time finding time to spend in the word and in prayer? Confront the problem and reevaluate your priorities.

Is the image of who God is clouded in your mind?
Get a new picture and hold on to it.

Has sin tried to creep in and take control of your mind?
Get in touch with the power of the Holy Spirit and do not let go.

Is doubt and confusion trying to reign and rule over your life? Get in the altar of God and do not move until something happens.

Step out in the river, friend. Step out into the river.

This old song says it well:

"Step into the water,
wade out a little bit deeper.
Wet your feet in the water of his love.
Ohh, Step into the water (children)
Wade out a little bit deeper,
come join angels singin',
praises to the Lamb of God.

It's time we the people,
stand up for what is right.
It's time we squared our shoulders back,
and raised our swords to fight.
For the Bible is our weapon,
and the spirit is my sheild.
The church needs more of its members to be workers in the field.

There is victory for the Christian,
who walks the narrow way.
There has been a prize appointed,
for the soul who does not stray.
Oh I want to live for Jesus,
be all that I should be.
So that I can rest with him forever,
live eternally."

2. The second thing about standing in the river:

John 7:37-38
In the last day, that great day of the feast, Jesus stood and cried, saying, If any man thirst, let him come unto me, and drink. He that believeth on me, as the scripture hath said, out of his belly shall flow rivers of living water.

There are so many times we question whether God has a miracle just for us? These are the times we need to step out into the river of the Holy Spirit and allow Him to speak to our heart and minister the truth into our life.

One of the signs of a maturing Christian is that, even when it doesn't feel like it, we can still know that we are in the river.

Our emotions are not being stirred, but we can still know that we are in the river.
The Holy Ghost goose bumps are not there, but we still know that we are in the river.

We may even feel like there is a barrier between us and the Lord, but we have that internal confidence that He is still right there with us guiding and teaching, and that in the end we will be refreshed by the river of His Spirit.

3. If we really want to see God do great and amazing miracles in our life we have to follow His Presence.

Joshua 3:11
Behold, the ark of the covenant of the Lord of all the earth passeth over before you into Jordan.

We need to have the attitude that Moses had in Exodus 33:15,

Exodus 33:15
And he said unto him, If thy presence go not with me, carry us not up hence.

What was Moses saying?
 "Lord, I am not going anywhere that You will not go. I know that You will never lead me into anything that is not good and nurturing and wholesome, because You have my best interest in mind. So, where You go, Lord, I will follow. But if You don't go, I don't want to go it alone."

Why was Paul's ministry so successful?

In his own mind, it seemed more cost effective and less time consuming to go into Asia and Bythinia to preach the gospel.

Bu,t when the Lord spoke to him in a dream about going to Macedonia he went. Because of his obedience, he then founded a church that would provide financial support for his ministry for years to come.

Look at what happens in God's presence.

Leviticus 9:23-24
And Moses and Aaron went into the tabernacle of the congregation, and came out, and blessed the people: and the glory of the Lord appeared unto all the people. And there came a fire out from before the Lord, and consumed

upon the altar the burnt offering and the fat: which when all the people saw, they shouted, and fell on their faces.

They saw the presence of God manifested because they were following the direction of God. If you are following the Lord, and you are seeking after Him, He has promised He will be found of you.

Jeremiah 29:13
And ye shall seek me, and find me, when ye shall search for me with all your heart.

4. How can we experience the great miracles of God? By trusting in His Word.

Joshua 3:13
And it shall come to pass, as soon as the soles of the feet of the priests that bear the ark of the Lord, the Lord of all the earth, shall rest in the waters of Jordan, that the waters of Jordan shall be cut off from the waters that come down from above; and they shall stand upon an heap.

There is absolutely no way under natural law that this was going to happen.

How would you have responded if you had been one of the priests carrying the Ark? "I don't think so Joshua. You go on ahead and test the waters. If it's OK then we'll come!"

That is one of the problems with the world today.
We are so pragmatic.
So many people will not believe what they cannot see.
We have been so influenced by the world.

The world says that the word cancer is a death sentence so we do not trust God for healing.

The world says that people are the products of their own doing so we do not offer help.

The world says that people will never change, so we keep the gospel to ourselves.

God's word says that healing is ours, that we become new creations after we are saved and that God so loved the world – everyone.

God's Word should be the compass that the church follows, leading us to the promises of God. The promises that He has given to each of us. Even when it does not make sense to us.

Trusting in His Word is faith.

Faith is when we quit believing what we see and start seeing what we believe.
Faith and trust enables us to receive the salvation of God.
Faith and trust enables us to receive the promises of God.
Faith and trust enables us to receive the blessings of God.
Faith and trust enables us to keep the commands of God.
We should not be moved by what we see.
We should not be moved by what we feel.
We should be moved by faith and trust in God's Word.

We can ask and keep on asking just like Jesus said we are to do but when it comes right down to it are we really trusting God to do what His word says He will do?

Luke 8:19-21
*Then came to him his mother and his brethren, and could not come at him for the press. And it was told him by certain which said, Thy mother and thy brethren stand without, desiring to see thee. And he answered and said unto them, My mother and my brethren are these **which hear the word of God, and do it.*** (Emphasis of author in bold).

That leads us to our next point.

5. How do we see God's miracle working power once again? We step out on faith.

Joshua 3:15
And as they that bare the ark were come unto Jordan, and the feet of the priests that bare the ark were dipped in the brim of the water, (for Jordan overfloweth all his banks all the time of harvest,)

Let's look at Luke 18:8

Luke 18:8
I tell you that he will avenge them speedily. Nevertheless when the Son of man cometh, shall he find faith on the earth?

What is Jesus talking about here?
He is not talking about saving faith, because when He returns He will take the church back to heaven for a marriage supper.

He is talking about the faith that it takes to:
know God's Word,

believe God's Word,
stand on God's Word,
walk in God's Word,
to step out on God's word in order to transform our surroundings.

If the church will ever grab hold of that, we will be in the midst of the greatest revival the world has ever known.

And maybe we are.

We tend to look at everything from an American perspective while around the world the Holy Spirit is moving as never before.

Churches are being built in unprecedented numbers.

People are being saved at astronomical rates.

They are receiving the Holy Ghost baptism with the evidence of speaking in other tongues as the Spirit gives them utterance by the thousands.

In any given 24 hour period: in China 30,000 people are coming to Christ, in Sub-Saharan Africa 20,000, and in Central and South America 10,000.

Why is that? Because God's people are penetrating the world with His word that is being confirmed by signs and wonders and miracles on a daily basis.

Even when it doesn't make any sense to take the Gospel into Muslim countries, churches are being established.

Even though it looks as if the enemy has established control over Africa, people are being healed and delivered from disease and false religion.

Now the Jordan is at flood stage all during harvest. Yet, as soon as the priests who carried the Ark reached the Jordan and their feet touched the water's edge, the water from upstream stopped flowing.

It piled up in a heap a great distance away, at a town called Adam in the vicinity of Zarethan, while the water flowing down to the Sea of the Arabah (the Salt Sea) was completely cut off.

God is waiting for us to step out in that kind of faith to receive our miracle.

6. If we are going to see God's miracle working power once again, we are going to have to cross over to the promise.

Joshua 3:16
*That the waters which came down from above stood and rose up upon an heap very far from the city Adam, that is beside Zaretan: and those that came down toward the sea of the plain, even the salt sea, failed, and were cut off: **and the people passed over right against Jericho**.*

I heard a great illustration about this very thing the other day and it refers to how the closer we get to our miracle the harder the enemy will work to defend his territory.

In football the hardest yards to cover are the last twenty yards before the goal line. It is called the Red Zone. You

see, the closer you get to reaching the goal the more
stubborn the enemy gets to keep you from getting it.
There are far more touchdowns that are scored from
grinding it out on the ground on one yard plunges than 50
yard passes.

How many of us, by faith, know that we have received our
miracle but we just haven't seen the manifestation of it
yet?
We know God's Word.
We stand God's Word.
We act God's Word.
But, we just haven't realized the fullness of the promise
yet. Why?

Football players give up because they haven't totally
bought into the head coach's offensive scheme, "We have
tried this before and it didn't work". Or they have become
so tired from grinding out 3-4 yards at a time that they just
do not have the strength to finish. So, they just give up and
give out before the end zone.

I have seen so many pastors that give up when their
blessing was just in reach.

I have seen so many Christians give up right before they
cross the finish line.

Or, they lose sight of the goal, because they consider it a
hopeless situation.

Or, the enemy wants to keep them out more than they want
to receive the promise.

Hebrews 12:1-3
Wherefore seeing we also are compassed about with so great a cloud of witnesses, let us lay aside every weight, and the sin which doth so easily beset us, and let us run with patience the race that is set before us, Looking unto Jesus the author and finisher of our faith; who for the joy that was set before him endured the cross, despising the shame, and is set down at the right hand of the throne of God. For consider him that endured such contradiction of sinners against himself, lest ye be wearied and faint in your minds.

7. If we really want to see the miracle of God and receive the miracle of God we are going to have to stand firm.

The priests, who carried the Ark of the Covenant of the LORD, stood firm on dry ground in the middle of the Jordan while all Israel passed by; until the whole nation had completed the crossing on dry ground. As the priests stood there waiting for Israel to cross on a dry riverbed, don't you know that they were aware of what was happening upstream from them?

The waters were piling up higher and higher. You could see it from where they were. Yet they never wavered. They knew that the One who had promised was able to see it through to the end.

I have heard testimonies of people who received complete healing only to be fooled again by the father of all lies who told them that nothing had changed. People have lost their healing, their blessing, and even their testimony because they failed to stand firm in the Lord.

Ephesians 6:10-13
Finally, my brethren, be strong in the Lord, and in the power of his might. Put on the whole armour of God, that ye may be able to stand against the wiles of the devil. For we wrestle not against flesh and blood, but against principalities, against powers, against the rulers of the darkness of this world, against spiritual wickedness in high places. Wherefore take unto you the whole armour of God, that ye may be able to withstand in the evil day, and having done all, to stand.

In Joshua 3:17 and in Ephesians 6:13 the words that are translated "stood firm" (Hebrew) and "stand" (Greek) both have the same alternate translation.

Both words mean, "to abide". So, once you have received your promise, your healing, your miracle, don't just see it but abide in it; live in it. Take possession of it and stay there. Don't let the devil force you out. He cannot unless you allow it.

1. Consecrate yourself

2. Stand in the river

3. Follow God's presence

4. Trust God's word

5. Step out in faith

6. Cross over into the promise

7. Stand firm.

Mark 5:25-34,
And a certain woman, which had an issue of blood twelve years, And had suffered many things of many physicians, and had spent all that she had, and was nothing bettered, but rather grew worse, When she had heard of Jesus, came in the press behind, and touched his garment. For she said, If I may touch but his clothes, I shall be whole. And straightway the fountain of her blood was dried up; and she felt in her body that she was healed of that plague. And Jesus, immediately knowing in himself that virtue had gone out of him, turned him about in the press, and said, Who touched my clothes? And his disciples said unto him, Thou seest the multitude thronging thee, and sayest thou, Who touched me? And he looked round about to see her that had done this thing. But the woman fearing and trembling, knowing what was done in her, came and fell down before him, and told him all the truth. And he said unto her, Daughter, thy faith hath made thee whole; go in peace, and be whole of thy plague.

This woman did everything she needed to do in order to receive her miracle and Jesus told her to "Go in peace…"

Is that what you need in your life today?

Chapter 2

Consecrated Living

Romans 8:1-17

Romans 8:1-17
There is therefore now no condemnation to them which are in Christ Jesus, who walk not after the flesh, but after the Spirit. For the law of the Spirit of life in Christ Jesus hath made me free from the law of sin and death. For what the law could not do, in that it was weak through the flesh, God sending his own Son in the likeness of sinful flesh, and for sin, condemned sin in the flesh: That the righteousness of the law might be fulfilled in us, who walk not after the flesh, but after the Spirit. For they that are after the flesh do mind the things of the flesh; but they that are after the Spirit the things of the Spirit. For to be carnally minded is death; but to be spiritually minded is life and peace. Because the carnal mind is enmity against God: for it is not subject to the law of God, neither indeed can be. So then they that are in the flesh cannot please God. But ye are not in the flesh, but in the Spirit, if so be that the Spirit of God dwell in you. Now if any man have not the Spirit of Christ, he is none of his. And if Christ be in you, the body is dead because of sin; but the Spirit is life because of righteousness. But if the Spirit of him that raised up Jesus from the dead dwell in you, he that raised up Christ from the dead shall also quicken your mortal bodies by his Spirit that dwelleth in you. Therefore, brethren, we are debtors, not to the flesh, to live after the flesh. For if ye live after the flesh, ye shall die: but if ye through the Spirit do mortify the deeds of the body, ye shall live. For as many as are led by the Spirit of God, they are the sons of God. For ye have not received the spirit of bondage again to fear; but ye have received the Spirit of adoption, whereby we cry, Abba, Father. The Spirit itself beareth witness with our spirit, that we are the children of God: And if children, then heirs; heirs of God, and joint-heirs with Christ; if so be that we suffer with him, that we may

be also glorified together.

If you expect to receive God's promised miracles in your life you need to consecrate yourself to Him and His purpose for you. God cannot bless a dirty vessel.

How can we consecrate ourselves to the Lord? What does that mean? When a person or thing was consecrated in the Old Testament, it was set apart for God's purpose. Priests were consecrated for work in the temple. Vessels were consecrated for use in temple worship.

So how are we to consecrate ourselves for the service of the Lord?

As Israel prepared to go into the Promised Land, Joshua told the people, "Consecrate yourselves, for tomorrow the LORD will do amazing things among you." I want to ask you, "Are you ready for God to do amazing things?"

We understand this consecration… to be an act that the people would willingly perform….. in order to be in right standing with God before they crossed the river.

Consecration, however, is more than just following the Law of God.

Consecration takes place in the heart and it makes one ready for whatever God wants to do in your life.

The Hebrew word means "to make holy" or "to prepare oneself".

When we consecrate ourselves to the Lord, we are telling God "I am making myself available to what you want for my life and not what I want."

It means a willingness to do what God specifically has for you and you alone.

God has set each of us apart for a specific purpose.

God has ordained His people to be the recipients of miracles, signs, and wonders – God's promises.
But, in order for us to receive the promise, we must first begin by consecrating ourselves. According to Romans 8:1-17 that takes place four ways.

1. Consecrated through your relationship with Jesus Christ.

2. Consecrated by living in the Spirit.

3. Consecrated by crucifying the flesh.

4. Consecrated by knowing who you are in Christ.

Now, before any of the following can take place, you must have repented of your sins. Turned away from them. That is number one. Secondly, you must be baptized in the name of Jesus for the remission of your sins so that you might receive the promise of the Holy Ghost. If you have repented of your sins, and been baptized in the name of Jesus for the remission of your sins, you can continue. If not this is the first thing you need to do.

This now being done, lets continue on. How can you be consecrated?

1. We are consecrated thorough our relationship with Jesus Christ.

Romans 8:1-4
There is therefore now no condemnation to them which are in Christ Jesus, who walk not after the flesh, but after the Spirit. For the law of the Spirit of life in Christ Jesus hath made me free from the law of sin and death. For what the law could not do, in that it was weak through the flesh, God sending his own Son in the likeness of sinful flesh, and for sin, condemned sin in the flesh: That the righteousness of the law might be fulfilled in us, who walk not after the flesh, but after the Spirit.

Paul begins this section of his letter to the church in Rome by saying:

Romans 8:1
Therefore, there is now no condemnation for those who are in Christ Jesus…

I believe that there are millions of well - intentioned church people today who think they are consecrated and sanctified because of the things they do.

They go to church. They teach Sunday School. They put money in the offering. They sing in the choir.

They have made a conscious choice to do all these good things.

But Paul tells us something quite different. Our consecration and sanctification does not come by our works.

Consecration and sanctification comes from being in Christ. It is based on our relationship with Christ.

Romans 8:2
because through Christ Jesus the law of the Spirit of life set me free from the law of sin and death.

In other words, what has been done in the spirit man, by the Spirit of Christ, has now taken precedence over what we have been trying to do by being good enough to please a holy God.

When we accept Christ as our Lord and Savior we are now set apart or consecrated to God by the Holy Spirit.

It is not some false sense of security we get by being satisfied with ourselves because of our good deeds.

That is why Paul makes a distinction between the law of the Spirit of life.

The law of the Spirit life is the grace which takes place in the spirit man.
We have nothing to do with it apart from staying in Christ. It is all based on our relationship with Christ.

The law of sin and death is good works that originate in the soul of a man. The law of sin and death is man trying to work his way to be good enough. Man will never be good enough to be holy, righteous, and sanctified through his works. It is by being in Christ.

Romans 8:3

For what the law was powerless to do in that it was weakened by the sinful nature, God did by sending his own Son in the likeness of sinful man to be a sin offering.

In Leviticus 20:7-8 the Lord told Moses to tell the Israelites,

Leviticus 20:7-8
Sanctify yourselves therefore, and be ye holy: for I am the Lord your God. And ye shall keep my statutes, and do them: I am the Lord which sanctify you.

"I am the Lord which sanctify you"... It is God that does the sanctifying.

This is a key point in consecration and sanctification.

Ephesians 2:8-9
For by grace are ye saved through faith; and that not of yourselves: it is the gift of God: Not of works, lest any man should boast.

It is the Lord who makes us holy.

It is the Lord who sets us apart.

It is the Lord who sanctifies us.

Consecration and Sanctification is a work that come by us being in Christ. It is based on our relationship with Christ.

Ephesians 2:10

For we are his workmanship, created in Christ Jesus unto good works, which God hath before ordained that we should walk in them.

What part do we play in our consecration?
What part do we play in our sanctification?

We are willing participants who desire to please God and to carry out the work that He has set before us. But, it is not the work that consecrates us or sanctifies us, it is being in Christ.

Romans 8:3-4
For what the law could not do, in that it was weak through the flesh, God sending his own Son in the likeness of sinful flesh, and for sin, condemned sin in the flesh:
That the righteousness of the law might be fulfilled in us, who walk not after the flesh, but after the Spirit.

Our consecration and our sanctification comes by staying in Christ; walking after the Spirit.

As long as we are in Christ, we are being consecrated.
As long as we are in Christ we are being sanctified.

It is when we get out of Chris that we begin to once again become entangled with the world and no longer separated unto Him.
How do we get out of Christ? Sin.

A holy God cannot stand in the presence of sin.

But, again, when we are in Christ, He will keep us out of sin, if we follow the leading of the Holy Spirit.

When the Holy Spirit says,
"Don't do that;
Don't go there;
Don't say that." We must listen and obey His command.

The way to stay in Christ is to not only listen to the Holy
Spirit but to obey the Holy Spirit. Hallelujah!

Let me ask you.
How is your relationship with Christ? Do you hear His
voice? Are you walking with Him daily? Is He real to you
and not just a great person in History?
Are you living the legend of Christ, or is He Lord of your
life today?

How are we consecrated?
1- Through our relationship with Christ.

2. We are consecrated and sanctified by Living According to the Spirit.

Now, with eternity in mind let us consider how being set
apart for the Lord affects us in this life.

Romans 8:5
*For they that are after the flesh do mind the things of the
flesh; but they that are after the Spirit the things of the
Spirit.*

What is Paul saying?

"Those who live according to the sinful nature have their minds set on what that nature desires; but those who live in accordance with the Spirit have their minds set on what the Spirit desires".
There are three parts to a man – body, soul and spirit.
Two of those parts are non-physical – the soul and the spirit.
It is out of one of these two areas of your being that moves your physical body to do what it does.

If you are operating out of the sinful nature or the "soul man" (remember that the soul is the mind, emotions, and personality – the non-physical area of natural man) then the acts of that sin nature will manifest itself in the body.

The acts of the sinful nature are not always seen as sinful acts in our lives, but they are sin, nonetheless.
Those acts come from what we think of as right without consideration for what God thinks is right.

That is where the Law of Moses failed. It satisfied the natural man, but it never satisfied the righteous requirements of the Law which is perfect adherence.

The law was kept, not out of love, but out of duty. This was why they were not able to keep the law. Their heart was not in it.

However, if you are living according to the Spirit, having the heart of the Spirit and the mind of the Spirit, your physical body will be doing the things of the Spirit, following the ways of the Spirit, and controlled by the Spirit.

We do not do the things we do to obtain righteousness, but, because we have been made righteous through Christ.

2 Peter 1:3-4
According as his divine power hath given unto us all things that pertain unto life and godliness, through the knowledge of him that hath called us to glory and virtue: Whereby are given unto us exceeding great and precious promises: that by these ye might be partakers of the divine nature, having escaped the corruption that is in the world through lust.

I have known people that, before they came to Christ, they went to church and tried to be good in hope that they could somehow earn their way to heaven. But, they never had assurance.

However, after they trust in Jesus Christ for their salvation, all doubt about their eternal destiny leaves them, because they have received eternal life through faith in Jesus.

Before, their salvation was works oriented.
Now, it is grace oriented.

Romans 8:6
For to be carnally minded is death; but to be spiritually minded is life and peace.

So consecration involves committing ourselves to Christ and then living according to the Spirit. Those who belong to Christ have the Holy Spirit dwelling in them – not because of some ritual that was performed but because of an act of grace we have received.

Romans 8:7
Because the carnal mind is enmity against God: for it is
not subject to the law of God, neither indeed can be.
Paul says in 1 Corinthians, chapter 2, that the man without
the Spirit of God cannot understand spiritual things
because they are only spiritually understood.
The same applies here.

Romans 8:8
So then they that are in the flesh cannot please God.

We cannot live a consecrated and sanctified life unless we
have the Holy Spirit guiding us and leading us. However,
it is not enough that the Spirit guides us and leads us. We
have to be willing to follow.

Are you following?
Are you allowing the Holy Spirit to have control?
Who is in control of your life?
Who is in control of your family?
Who is in control of your future?
Who is in control of your resources?
Who is in control of everything you are, have and plan on
being and doing?

How are we consecrated and sanctified?
Consecration and sanctification comes:
1. Through our relationship with Christ.
2. By living according to the Spirit, being led by and
following the Spirit.

3. Consecration and sanctification come by Crucifying the Flesh.

How do you crucify the flesh?
It comes by changing the way you think.
Instead of thinking from the natural man perspective, you
begin to think from a spiritual mindset.

What is God speaking to you?
What is the Holy Spirit leading you to?
Crucifying the flesh means that we have learned to submit
to His will for your life in every circumstance.

Romans 8:9
*But ye are not in the flesh, but in the Spirit, if so be that the
Spirit of God dwell in you. Now if any man have not the
Spirit of Christ, he is none of his.*

I want you to understand clearly what Paul is warning
against here. If the Spirit of God dwells in you through
salvation then the fruit of the Spirit will be evident in your
life.

It is a conscious decision we make to allow the Holy Spirit
of God to have complete control.

When the Spirit of God is in control of a person's life, we
do not look at the fruit of the Spirit and pick out which one
you want or decide which one you need to work on.

But, if you belong to Christ, each of the fruits of the Spirit
that is mentioned will build upon the other so that our life
will be a reflection of the Spirit inside of us.

The fact is that the fruit of the Spirit is already planted in us when we are saved. It is up to us to allow them to be seen in our life.

Again, the change is one that has taken place inwardly and is expected to be seen outwardly.

Romans 8:10
And if Christ be in you, the body is dead because of sin; but the Spirit is life because of righteousness.

Crucifying the flesh, then, is not just putting an end to bad things in your life, but, it also means that we stop trying to do the things that God has already done.

We cannot earn salvation – it is already done.
We cannot be good enough to receive healing – by His stripes you are healed.
We cannot ever be perfect enough for God to supply all our needs—He has already done that.

Crucifying the flesh means accepting, by faith, the things that God has already provided for us. Glory, Glory, Glory!

Romans 8:11
But if the Spirit of him that raised up Jesus from the dead dwell in you, he that raised up Christ from the dead shall also quicken your mortal bodies by his Spirit that dwelleth in you.

Romans 1:4 says that it is the power of the Holy Spirit that raised Jesus from the dead.

It is the same power that is at work in us:

to resurrect a dead spirit,
to give us life,
to give us unwavering faith.
It is the same power working in us helping us receive
every promise that has been given us.

Jeremiah 29:11-14
For I know the thoughts that I think toward you, saith the LORD, thoughts of peace, and not of evil, to give you an expected end. Then shall ye call upon me, and ye shall go and pray unto me, and I will hearken unto you. And ye shall seek me, and find me, when ye shall search for me with all your heart. And I will be found of you, saith the LORD: and I will turn away your captivity, and I will gather you from all the nations, and from all the places whither I have driven you, saith the LORD; and I will bring you again into the place whence I caused you to be carried away captive.

How are we consecrated?
1. Through our relationship with Christ.
2. By living according to the Spirit.
3. By Crucifying the Flesh.

4. By Living as an Heir to God's Promises.

It is not enough to know God's promises, but we have to live as an Heir to those promises.

I want to quickly go through a few main points that Paul is trying to make.

1) If we are consecrated and sanctified unto God we have
an obligation to God.

Galatians 2:20
I am crucified with Christ: nevertheless I live; yet not I,
but Christ liveth in me: and the life which I now live in the
flesh I live by the faith of the Son of God, who loved me,
and gave himself for me.

The only thing that you can do in response to what God
has done for you is to give your life back to Him.

Romans 8:13
For if ye live after the flesh, ye shall die: but if ye through
the Spirit do mortify the deeds of the body, ye shall live.

2) If we are consecrated and sanctified unto God we are
God's child.

Romans 8:14
For as many as are led by the Spirit of God, they are the
sons of God.

The importance of being God's child is that you have now
become heirs to all of God's promises.

Healing, miracles, signs and wonders, blessing, financial
security… they all belong to those who trust Him and are
obedient to His word.

3) If you are consecrated and sanctified unto God you can
have confidence instead of fear because God is your
Father.

Romans 8:15
For ye have not received the spirit of bondage again to
fear; but ye have received the Spirit of adoption, whereby
we cry, Abba, Father. The Spirit itself beareth witness with
our spirit, that we are the children of God:

4) If you are consecrated to God then you are co=-heirs
with Christ.
That means that everything that the Father has given Jesus
is also yours.

Ephesians 2:6
And hath raised us up together, and made us sit together in
heavenly places in Christ Jesus:

So if we are seated with Jesus right now in the heavenlies
we have eternal life,
we have power,
we have authority,
and we have every promise that has been given to the
church.

I want to close with this.
We are talking about 7 steps to receiving all God's
promises according to Joshua 3.

1. Consecrate yourself

2. Stand in the river

3. Follow God's presence

4. Trust God's word

5. Step out in faith

6. Cross over into the promise

7. Stand firm.

The first step is that you must be saved. You need Jesus to take control of your life. That is the first step of the first step. As I spoke about being set apart for God, some of what I spoke of was about salvation. Salvation is for your eternal life. But much of what I spoke of was about your life in Christ right here and right now. God desires that we live lives that are reflective of His nature and not our fallen nature. When we are born again we receive the Holy Spirit to bear witness that we are God's children. But there is something else that God desires for your life. It is the power to live the life that we are called to. It is the mighty baptism in the Holy Spirit that Jesus said would come to those who ask.

Acts 1:8,
But you will receive power when the Holy Spirit comes on you; and you will be my witnesses in Jerusalem, and in all Judea and Samaria, and to the ends of the earth.

If salvation is for eternity then the baptism in the Holy Spirit is for this life right here and right now.
It is the power you need to live your life for Jesus.
It is the fire you need to burn for Jesus.
It is the revelation you need to go deeper in the word of God. It is the illumination you need to understand the word.

Salvation sets you apart from the world. The baptism in the Holy Spirit sets you apart while you are in the world.

If you do not know Jesus as your Lord and Savior, and you do not have the assurance of heaven, you need to make that decision today. There may not be a tomorrow.

If you know Jesus and want to go deeper, you need to ask Him to baptize you in the Holy Spirit. He will pour out the Spirit into your life today.

God wants to set you apart for eternity and for now by His Holy Spirit.

Will you allow Him to do that today?

Chapter 3

Stand in the River

Ezekiel 47:1-12

The baptism of the Holy Spirit prepares you for God's promised miracles.

So far, we have seen that the first step to receiving God's promised miracles is to consecrate yourself. That means setting yourself apart from the worldly desires and the lusts of the flesh and to allow God to have pre-eminence in your life.

The second step, as told to Israel by Joshua, 'stand in the river'.

As has already been mentioned, the main work in consecration or sanctification is separating yourself from sin by giving your life to Jesus Christ. It is the repenting of your sin, and being baptized in Jesus name for the remission of your sin, that prepares you to be the temple of the Holy Spirit.

There is no other way to be set apart from the world. That is the first step and it is God's grace at work in your life. Interestingly enough, the second step is also an act of grace, and like the first act it requires that the recipient ask for it.

It is the baptism in the Holy Spirit and is available to all the saved who ask for it. After you have been baptized in the name of Jesus you are making yourself ready for the Holy Spirit.

Acts 2:38-39
Then Peter said unto them, Repent, and be baptized every one of you in the name of Jesus Christ for the remission of

sins, and ye shall receive the gift of the Holy Ghost. For the promise is unto you, and to your children, and to all that are afar off, even as many as the LORD our God shall call.

Have you ever gone to the gas station to fill up - you know your tank is about empty so you put the nozzle in to start it. The next thing you know the automatic shut off kicks in at about eight gallons.

You know your tank holds sixteen gallons. So what is your next move? Do you take the nozzle out and say, "Well, I guess that is all God wants me to have today. I'll try again some other time." Or, do you say, "I came to get filled up and I am not leaving here until I am!" That is the attitude that God wants you to have. That is why He told the Israelites, even though it did not make any sense, to go stand in the river.

Jesus said, "But you will receive power when the Holy Spirit comes on you; and you will be my witnesses in Jerusalem, and in all Judea and Samaria, and to the ends of the earth."

<u>1. Notice the source of the River</u>

Ezekiel 47:1-12
Afterward he brought me again unto the door of the house; and, behold, waters issued out from under the threshold of the house eastward: for the forefront of the house stood toward the east, and the waters came down from under from the right side of the house, at the south side of the altar. Then brought he me out of the way of the gate

northward, and led me about the way without unto the utter gate by the way that looketh eastward; and, behold, there ran out waters on the right side. And when the man that had the line in his hand went forth eastward, he measured a thousand cubits, and he brought me through the waters; the waters were to the ankles. Again he measured a thousand, and brought me through the waters; the waters were to the knees. Again he measured a thousand, and brought me through; the waters were to the loins. Afterward he measured a thousand; and it was a river that I could not pass over: for the waters were risen, waters to swim in, a river that could not be passed over. And he said unto me, Son of man, hast thou seen this? Then he brought me, and caused me to return to the brink of the river. Now when I had returned, behold, at the bank of the river were very many trees on the one side and on the other. Then said he unto me, These waters issue out toward the east country, and go down into the desert, and go into the sea: which being brought forth into the sea, the waters shall be healed. And it shall come to pass, that every thing that liveth, which moveth, whithersoever the rivers shall come, shall live: and there shall be a very great multitude of fish, because these waters shall come thither: for they shall be healed; and every thing shall live whither the river cometh. And it shall come to pass, that the fishers shall stand upon it from Engedi even unto Eneglaim; they shall be a place to spread forth nets; their fish shall be according to their kinds, as the fish of the great sea, exceeding many. But the miry places thereof and the marishes thereof shall not be healed; they shall be given to salt. And by the river upon the bank thereof, on this side and on that side, shall grow all trees for meat, whose leaf shall not fade, neither shall the fruit thereof be consumed: it shall bring forth new fruit according to his months, because their waters they issued out of the sanctuary: and the fruit thereof shall be for meat, and the leaf thereof for medicine.

Some say that this is a picture of the Temple that will be built during the Millennial Reign of Christ.

Still others say it is symbolic of the Church, the temple of the Holy Spirit, both individually and corporately.

If you are the temple, in the light of what is flowing from it, you might think that the last interpretation is the right one. However, if you look at the river in connection with the description of the River in Revelation 22 we may begin to see something different.

Revelation 22:1-2
And he shewed me a pure river of water of life, clear as crystal, proceeding out of the throne of God and of the Lamb. In the midst of the street of it, and on either side of the river, was there the tree of life, which bare twelve manner of fruits, and yielded her fruit every month: and the leaves of the tree were for the healing of the nations.

Do you see the connection between the river as seen by Ezekiel and the River of Revelation? Now, about the temple…

Revelation 21:15-21
And he that talked with me had a golden reed to measure the city, and the gates thereof, and the wall thereof. And the city lieth foursquare, and the length is as large as the breadth: and he measured the city with the reed, twelve

thousand furlongs. The length and the breadth and the height of it are equal. And he measured the wall thereof, an hundred and forty and four cubits, according to the measure of a man, that is, of the angel. And the building of the wall of it was of jasper: and the city was pure gold, like unto clear glass. And the foundations of the wall of the city were garnished with all manner of precious stones. The first foundation was jasper; the second, sapphire; the third, a chalcedony; the fourth, an emerald; The fifth, sardonyx; the sixth, sardius; the seventh, chrysolyte; the eighth, beryl; the ninth, a topaz; the tenth, a chrysoprasus; the eleventh, a jacinth; the twelfth, an amethyst. And the twelve gates were twelve pearls: every several gate was of one pearl: and the street of the city was pure gold, as it were transparent glass.

John sees a picture and gives a beautiful description of the eternal city.

Revelation 21:22
And I saw no temple therein: for the Lord God Almighty and the Lamb are the temple of it.

So, let us look at it from that perspective. The Temple is the eternal temple of God. The Temple faces east but the River is flowing from the Temple on the south.
That means that the place where the river flows from is on the right side of the temple – right where Jesus is now – seated at the right hand of the Father. Since Jesus and the Father are one then this means that the power is coming from the right side. And it is the river of power that is flowing, the river of the Holy Spirit that is flowing. John the Baptist said in Mark 1:7-8

Mark 1:6-8
*And John was clothed with camel's hair, and with a girdle
of a skin about his loins; and he did eat locusts and wild
honey: And preached, saying, There cometh one mightier
than I after me, the latchet of whose shoes I am not worthy
to stoop down and unloose. I indeed have baptized you
with water: but he shall baptize you with the Holy Ghost.*

OK, so how do we make the connection between this river
that Ezekiel sees and the Holy Spirit? Jesus does that for
us.

John 7:37-39
*In the last day, that great day of the feast, Jesus stood and
cried, saying, If any man thirst, let him come unto me, and
drink. He that believeth on me, as the scripture hath said,
out of his belly shall flow rivers of living water. (But this
spake he of the Spirit, which they that believe on him
should receive: for the Holy Ghost was not yet given;
because that Jesus was not yet glorified.)*

The power of the Holy Spirit is available for those that will
seek it. It is pouring out today. Will you come under its
flow? It is flowing out of the throne of God. It is the
presence of God flowing from God on those that are
seeking to be touched by it.

2. Notice the depth of the river.

In verses 3-6, Ezekiel now describes four different levels
of encounter with the Holy Spirit.

Ezekiel 47:3-6
And when the man that had the line in his hand went forth

eastward, he measured a thousand cubits, and he brought me through the waters; the waters were to the ankles. Again he measured a thousand, and brought me through the waters; the waters were to the knees. Again he measured a thousand, and brought me through; the waters were to the loins. Afterward he measured a thousand; and it was a river that I could not pass over: for the waters were risen, waters to swim in, a river that could not be passed over. And he said unto me, Son of man, hast thou seen this? Then he brought me, and caused me to return to the brink of the river.

If you try to understand the River of the Holy Spirit as something that happens in a series of progressive moves as you grow in the Lord it would seem as though this first level of the river would be for entry level Christians – just the beginning of your life in the Spirit.

But I think there is more to it than that. Some seem to think that you can step in and try it out and if you don't like it you can just get out. Several years ago, some friends and I went to Hampton Beach in New Hampshire on the eastern coast of the USA. As soon as we got there, they kicked their shoes of and took off running for the water. Not me! The first thing I did was to bend down and feel the water to see if I wanted to get in it. And it was way too cold for me so I never got in. It was about ninety-five degrees that day but I chose to stay out of what would have refreshed me.

That is the way too many Christians are today. It doesn't matter that the Word of God says we should be baptized in the Spirit. They say, "It is not something that we grew up with", or, "I was never taught that", "I don't want anyone to think I've gone off the deep end", "I was raised this way or that and that is not what our church believes". Friend, this is not about what your local church believes. This is about you getting all that the Lord has for you in abundance. Jesus said in Luke 9:62:

Luke 9:62
And Jesus said unto him, No man, having put his hand to the plough, and looking back, is fit for the kingdom of God.

God wants you to take that initial step without concern for your comfort zone. God wants to take you further. God wants to take you deeper. There is so much more if you will just take His hand and go into the deeper parts with Him.

The reality is that the first three steps – ankle deep, knee deep and then waist deep, do not refer to the fullness of what God has for His people. The first three steps can only take you as far as you want to move in the Spirit after salvation. You see, after salvation you have to have a desire to move in the Spirit. You have to want a more intimate relationship with the risen Savior. But it just cannot happen by you treading around in the "kiddy pool". Am I saying that you can't draw closer to God after you are saved? Not at all! What I am saying is that when you are ankle deep, knee deep or waist deep your feet are on the ground. You are in control. You go where you want to go and do what you want to do in your own power.

Romans 8:5
For they that are after the flesh do mind the things of the

flesh; but they that are after the Spirit the things of the Spirit.

Those who live according to the sinful nature have their minds set on what that nature desires; but those who live in accordance with the Spirit have their minds set on what the Spirit desires.

Remember that the sinful nature isn't just about sin in your life. It is not about doing what seems right in your own eyes instead of being led by the Spirit, or trying to please God by what you do instead of accepting what He has already done.

You may say that you want to be led by the Spirit, but the only way to do that is to take the next step. God measured off another thousand, but, now, it was a river that Ezekial could not cross because the water had risen and was deep enough to swim in—a river that no one could cross.

"He asked me, 'Son of man, do you see this?' Notice that the man in the vision wanted to make sure that Ezekiel saw and understood what was taking place. God wants His people to experience the fullness of life in the Spirit.

Ephesians 3:16-19
That he would grant you, according to the riches of his glory, to be strengthened with might by his Spirit in the inner man; That Christ may dwell in your hearts by faith; that ye, being rooted and grounded in love, May be able to comprehend with all saints what is the breadth, and length, and depth, and height; And to know the love of Christ, which passeth knowledge, that ye might be filled with all the fulness of God.

Now look at Acts 19:1-7.

Acts 19:1-7.
And it came to pass, that, while Apollos was at Corinth, Paul having passed through the upper coasts came to Ephesus: and finding certain disciples, He said unto them, have ye received the Holy Ghost since ye believed? And they said unto him, we have not so much as heard whether there be any Holy Ghost. And he said unto them, unto what then were ye baptized? And they said, Unto John's baptism.
Then said Paul, John verily baptized with the baptism of repentance, saying unto the people, that they should believe on him which should come after him, that is, on Christ Jesus. When they heard this, they were baptized in the name of the Lord Jesus. And when Paul had laid his hands upon them, the Holy Ghost came on them; and they spake with tongues, and prophesied. And all the men were about twelve.

How important is the baptism in the Holy Spirit? Paul understood it to be of vital importance. While Apollos was at Corinth, Paul took the road through the interior and arrived at Ephesus. There he found some disciples and asked them, "Did you receive the Holy Spirit when you believed?"

They answered, "No, we have not even heard that there is a Holy Spirit."

So, Paul asked, "Then what baptism did you receive?"

"John's baptism," they replied.

Paul said, "John's baptism was a baptism of repentance. He told the people to believe in the one coming after him, that is, in Jesus." On hearing this, they were baptized into the name of the Lord Jesus. When Paul placed his hands on them, the Holy Spirit came on them, and they spoke in tongues and prophesied. There were about twelve men in all.

Paul knew that these men were saved; "he found some disciples" that believed. But, he knew they needed the baptism in the Holy Spirit. It was only after he had talked to them and determined them to be Christians that he took the next step. He baptized them in the name of Jesus and then laid his hands on them, and they received the Holy Spirit. What was the evidence? They spoke in other tongues... What points to tongues as evidence is that it is not something that occurs in the natural? It is out of the control of the individual, which is exactly what Ezekiel sees as God's desire for His people.

Acts 2:32-33
This Jesus hath God raised up, whereof we all are witnesses. Therefore being by the right hand of God exalted, and having received of the Father the promise of the Holy Ghost, he hath shed forth this, which ye now see and hear.

Please understand here that Jesus is not literally at the Father's right hand as Jesus and the Father are one. The right hand was often used by the Hebrews to mean power. God has raised this Jesus to life by His power. It was the power of the Spirit of God, since God is Spirit, that raised the humanity of God. One in the same and we are all witnesses of the fact.

The Father is pouring out of His Spirit. He wants to take us to the middle of the river where the current of the Spirit takes us where He wants to go. We submit totally to His will for our lives.

3. Notice is the effects of the river.

Ezekiel 47:7-12
Now when I had returned, behold, at the bank of the river were very many trees on the one side and on the other. 47:8 Then said he unto me, These waters issue out toward the east country, and go down into the desert, and go into the sea: which being brought forth into the sea, the waters shall be healed. 47:9 And it shall come to pass, that every thing that liveth, which moveth, whithersoever the rivers shall come, shall live: and there shall be a very great multitude of fish, because these waters shall come thither: for they shall be healed; and every thing shall live whither the river cometh. 47:10 And it shall come to pass, that the fishers shall stand upon it from Engedi even unto Eneglaim; they shall be a place to spread forth nets; their fish shall be according to their kinds, as the fish of the great sea, exceeding many. 47:11 But the miry places thereof and the marishes thereof shall not be healed; they shall be given to salt. 47:12 And by the river upon the bank thereof, on this side and on that side, shall grow all trees for meat, whose leaf shall not fade, neither shall the fruit thereof be consumed: it shall bring forth new fruit according to his months, because their waters they issued out of the sanctuary: and the fruit thereof shall be for meat, and the leaf thereof for medicine.

"Then he led me back to the bank of the river".

Verse 7

"When I arrived there, I saw a great number of trees on each side of the river".

Five effects of the river.

1). It brings freshness…

Verse 8

"He said to me, 'This water flows toward the eastern region and goes down into the Arabah, where it enters the sea'.

When it empties into the Sea, the water there becomes fresh.

Psalm 104:30
Thou sendest forth thy spirit, they are created: and thou renewest the face of the earth.

"When you send your Spirit, they are created, and you renew the face of the earth".

2) It brings life…

Verse 9
And it shall come to pass, that every thing that liveth, which moveth, whithersoever the rivers shall come, shall live: and there shall be a very great multitude of fish, because these waters shall come thither: for they shall be healed; and every thing shall live whither the river cometh.

Swarms of living creatures will live wherever the river flows. Jesus said in John 10:10, "The thief comes only to steal and kill and destroy; I have come that they may have life, and have it to the full". That is the abundant life that comes from the baptism in the Holy Spirit.

3) It attracts great numbers…

Verse 9
And it shall come to pass, that every thing that liveth, which moveth, whithersoever the rivers shall come, shall live: and there shall be a very great multitude of fish, because these waters shall come thither: for they shall be healed; and every thing shall live whither the river cometh.

"There will be large numbers of fish, because this water flows there and makes the salt water fresh; so where the river flows everything will live. The sick, the lame and the diseased will be healed".

John 6:2
And a great multitude followed him, because they saw his miracles which he did on them that were diseased.

4) It provides food…

Verse 10
And it shall come to pass, that the fishers shall stand upon it from Engedi even unto Eneglaim; they shall be a place to spread forth nets; their fish shall be according to their kinds, as the fish of the great sea, exceeding many.

Verse 12
*And by the river upon the bank thereof, on this side and on that side, shall grow all trees for meat, whose leaf shall not fade, neither shall the fruit thereof be consumed: it shall bring forth new fruit according to his months, because their waters they issued out of the sanctuary: and **the fruit thereof shall be for meat,** and the leaf thereof for medicine.*

"Fishermen will stand along the shore; from En Gedi to En Eglaim there will be places for spreading nets. The fish will be of many kinds—like the fish of the Great Sea. Fruit trees of all kinds will grow on both banks of the river. Their leaves will not wither, nor will their fruit fail. Every month they will bear, because the water from the sanctuary flows to them. Their fruit will serve for food…"

Jesus said that man does not live by bread alone but by every word that comes from the mouth of God… The baptism in the Holy Spirit will increase your hunger for the word and increase your understanding of the word.

5) It provides healing… 'their leaves for healing'.

Verse 12
*And by the river upon the bank thereof, on this side and on that side, shall grow all trees for meat, whose leaf shall not fade, neither shall the fruit thereof be consumed: it shall bring forth new fruit according to his months, because their waters they issued out of the sanctuary: and the fruit thereof shall be for meat, and the **leaf thereof for medicine**.*

Joshua told the Priests that step #2 was to go and stand in
the river. It was not until they were willing to do so that
they opened the door for a miracle.

Many times, I and a group of guys have gone up into the
mountains of North Carolina, a place called Linville
Gorge. There is a river that runs through the gorge with
some very deep pockets in it. These are places the water is
very deep. When we get up there some of us gently wade
into the water. This water is so cold. Others run out waist
deep. But the ones who impressed me the most were the
crazies who scrambled along a very narrow foot path,
holding on to whatever they could to get them over to a
rock outcropping, where they then jump or dive into the
deepest part of the river. They do not wade through ankle
deep water to get there. They go from the safety of land to
the frigid waters of the river where they are at the mercy of
the river. They do not look at the conditions - the depth,
the temperature or the height of the cliff. They just bailed
and squealed with delight all the way down.

Romans 14:17-18 says that is the way that we are
supposed to be.

Romans 14:17-18
For the kingdom of God is not meat and drink; but
righteousness, and peace, and joy in the Holy Ghost.
14:18 For he that in these things serveth Christ is
acceptable to God, and approved of men.

Is the baptism in the Holy Spirit with the evidence of speaking in other tongues for you?

Are you saved? Then it is for you.

Are you hungry? Then it is for you.

Are you willing to give the Holy Spirit control of your life? Then it is for you.

You may say, "Well, Brother George, I have things in my life that I need to get rid of first". The truth of the matter is that it is Holy Ghost power that you need in your life to get rid of those things. If you could do it on your own don't you think you would have?

Are you ready to stand in the River?

Friend, if you have repented and turned from your sins, been baptized in Jesus' name for the remission of your sins, then you are ready to receive the Holy Ghost.

Your life will never be the same.

Chapter 4

Follow God's Presence

Exodus 33:12-25

We should only want to go where God is. Our goal should be to follow Him wherever He might lead. Moses gives us an example of that.

Exodus 33:12-25
And Moses said unto the LORD, See, thou sayest unto me, Bring up this people: and thou hast not let me know whom thou wilt send with me. Yet thou hast said, I know thee by name, and thou hast also found grace in my sight. 33:13 Now therefore, I pray thee, if I have found grace in thy sight, show me now thy way, that I may know thee, that I may find grace in thy sight: and consider that this nation is thy people. 33:14 And he said, My presence shall go with thee, and I will give thee rest. 33:15 And he said unto him, If thy presence go not with me, carry us not up hence. 33:16 For wherein shall it be known here that I and thy people have found grace in thy sight? is it not in that thou goest with us? so shall we be separated, I and thy people, from all the people that are upon the face of the earth. 33:17 And the LORD said unto Moses, I will do this thing also that thou hast spoken: for thou hast found grace in my sight, and I know thee by name. 33:18 And he said, I beseech thee, show me thy glory. 33:19 And he said, I will make all my goodness pass before thee, and I will proclaim the name of the LORD before thee; and will be gracious to whom I will be gracious, and will show mercy on whom I will show mercy. 33:20 And he said, Thou canst not see my face: for there shall no man see me, and live. 33:21 And the LORD said, Behold, there is a place by me, and thou shalt stand upon a rock: 33:22 And it shall come to pass, while my glory passeth by, that I will put thee in a cleft of the rock, and will cover thee with my hand while I pass by: 33:23 And I will take away mine hand, and thou shalt see my back parts: but my face shall not be seen.

Dear friend, as you are studying this book, I want you to be sure that you understand something; this is not some prescribed ritual that you follow and when you are done, Poof! There is your miracle. It is more about your heart and attitudes toward God. I just wanted to clear that up. Now, let me say this. All of these steps are clearly described in Joshua 3 as seven steps that needed to occur before Israel could cross over into the Land of Promise.

As we go through, you may notice that the steps appear to be a natural progression of your relationship with Jesus Christ. I hope that you see it that way, for I believe that is how God intended it to be for His chosen people. So let us recap; Step 1 – Consecrate yourself, step 2 – Stand in the River, and now step 3 - Follow the Lord's Presence.

Joshua 3:11
Behold, the ark of the covenant of the LORD of all the earth passeth over before you into Jordan.

God tells Joshua, "See, the ark of the covenant of the Lord of all the earth will go into the Jordan ahead of you".

In order for us to follow God's presence in our lives we have to know who He is. I want to read a few letters that children wrote to God that reveal a cute but inadequate picture of who God is.

Dear God,
Thank you for the baby brother
but what I asked for was a puppy.
I never asked for anything before.
You can look it up.
Joyce

Dear God,
I read the Bible.
What does beget mean?
Nobody will tell me.
Love Alison

Dear God,
I bet it is very hard for you
to love all of everybody in the whole world.
There are only 4 people in our family
and I can never do it.
Nancy

Dear God,
My Grandpa says you were around
when he was a little boy.
How far back do you go?
Love, Dennis

Dear God,
How come you did all those miracles
in the old days and don't do any now?
Billy

Dear God,
Is Reverend Coe a friend of yours,
or do you just know him through the business?
Donny

Our Father who does art in heaven
Harold is His Name
Reese

And dear Lord forgive us our trash passes,

As we forgive those who passed trash against us
Wendy

And, saving the best for last.

Dear God,
I didn't think orange went with purple
until I saw the sunset
you made on Tuesday night.
That was really cool.
Thomas

I think Tomas has a pretty good picture in his mind of who
God is don't you.

Hebrews 5:11-14
Of whom we have many things to say, and hard to be
uttered, seeing ye are dull of hearing. 5:12 For when for
the time ye ought to be teachers, ye have need that one
teach you again which be the first principles of the oracles
of God; and are become such as have need of milk, and not
of strong meat. 5:13 For every one that useth milk is
unskilful in the word of righteousness: for he is a babe.
5:14 But strong meat belongeth to them that are of full
age, even those who by reason of use have their senses
exercised to discern both good and evil.

Let us take the time today to learn how to follow God's
presence in our lives.

<u>1. It is a must: That you remember God's call</u>

Exodus 33:12
And Moses said unto the LORD, See, thou sayest unto me, Bring up this people: and thou hast not let me know whom thou wilt send with me. Yet thou hast said, I know thee by name, and thou hast also found grace in my sight.

A. Notice the call.

Moses remembers the specific call that God has placed on his life.

He was the one who was to lead Israel into the Promised Land.
He was the one that God consecrated for that work.
He was the one upon whom God had placed His Spirit.

We know God placed His Spirit on Moses because Moses was a prophet and prophets only spoke as they were carried along by the Holy Spirit.

In verse 12, I want you to look at the word "know". The word translated "know" means to 'ascertain by seeing or by careful observation or instruction; understanding'. Moses wanted to see or be able to observe, be instructed by, and understand who it was that God was going to send along with him.

In order for us to understand what Moses is saying we have to go back to 33:1-3.

Exodus 33:1-3
And the LORD said unto Moses, Depart, and go up hence, thou and the people which thou hast brought up out of the

land of Egypt, unto the land which I sware unto Abraham, to Isaac, and to Jacob, saying, Unto thy seed will I give it: 33:2 And I will send an angel before thee; and I will drive out the Canaanite, the Amorite, and the Hittite, and the Perizzite, the Hivite, and the Jebusite: 33:3 Unto a land flowing with milk and honey: for I will not go up in the midst of thee; for thou art a stiffnecked people: lest I consume thee in the way.

B. Notice the Connection.

Moses was not going to be satisfied with an angel leading the way. He wanted God to go ahead of Him. He wanted to know God in the same way he understood God knew him; 'I know you by name…'

Jeremiah 1:5
Before I formed thee in the belly I knew thee; and before thou camest forth out of the womb I sanctified thee, and I ordained thee a prophet unto the nations.

Moses understood that God had placed a call on his life. But he was not satisfied with going on without the Lord's presence. He had to have that connection through the visible manifestation of God in order to finish what he was called to do.

C. Next, notice the Craving.

Exodus 13:33
Before I formed thee in the belly I knew thee; and before thou camest forth out of the womb I sanctified thee, and I ordained thee a prophet unto the nations.

This should be the heart cry of every believer.

1) 'If you are pleased with me…' The word "if" may be more appropriately translated as "since". There is only one way for God to be pleased with you and that is through a relationship with Jesus Christ.

Hebrews 11:24-29
By faith Moses, when he was come to years, refused to be called the son of Pharaoh's daughter; 11:25 Choosing rather to suffer affliction with the people of God, than to enjoy the pleasures of sin for a season; 11:26 Esteeming the reproach of Christ greater riches than the treasures in Egypt: for he had respect unto the recompence of the reward. 11:27 By faith he forsook Egypt, not fearing the wrath of the king: for he endured, as seeing him who is invisible. 11:28 Through faith he kept the passover, and the sprinkling of blood, lest he that destroyed the firstborn should touch them. 11:29 By faith they passed through the Red sea as by dry land: which the Egyptians assaying to do were drowned.

2) 'Teach me your ways so I may know you and continue to find favor with you…'

Teaching is the ministry of the Holy Spirit. Not only does the Holy Spirit teach but He also sustains us in our faith. One thing that the baptism in the Holy Spirit does is to give you a renewed hunger for the word of God. You will be able to pray more and stay in the Word more. You will not be satisfied.

3) 'Remember that this nation is your people…' As God's people you have the legal right under the new covenant to

expect God to be faithful to His promises through that covenant. If the covenant promises are not being seen it is never because God has broken His part of the agreement.

<u>2. It is a must: that you recognize God's Presence.</u>

Exodus 33:14
And he said, My presence shall go with thee, and I will give thee rest.

One of the things that has been difficult for me to understand is how the nation of Israel, some 3 million strong, could stumble through the wilderness with the visible presence of the Living God in the middle of their camp, a cloud by day and a pillar of fire by night, being visible from everywhere, and still grumble and complain their way out of the Promise. Yet, the more I read, the more revelation I get. The Israelites saw the cloud and the fire. They knew that it was God. But, they didn't know God. And it was that lack of a relationship that created a barrier for them and kept them from really recognizing the significance of God's manifest presence in the camp.

Look back at verse 5.

Exodus 33:5-6
For the LORD had said unto Moses, Say unto the children of Israel, Ye are a stiffnecked people: I will come up into the midst of thee in a moment, and consume thee: therefore now put off thy ornaments from thee, that I may know what to do unto thee. And the children of Israel stripped themselves of their ornaments by the mount Horeb.

The ornaments that they wore were the jewelry and precious things that had been given them by the Egyptians as they were leaving their captivity. Now, according to verse 6, it appears that there was a change of heart because the people took those ornaments off. But it seems as though that was only outward in appearance and not an inward work, because God was still not pleased with them.

Exodus 33:7-10
And Moses took the tabernacle, and pitched it without the camp, afar off from the camp, and called it the Tabernacle of the congregation. And it came to pass, that every one which sought the LORD went out unto the tabernacle of the congregation, which was without the camp. 33:8 And it came to pass, when Moses went out unto the tabernacle, that all the people rose up, and stood every man at his tent door, and looked after Moses, until he was gone into the tabernacle. 33:9 And it came to pass, as Moses entered into the tabernacle, the cloudy pillar descended, and stood at the door of the tabernacle, and the Lord talked with Moses. 33:10 And all the people saw the cloudy pillar stand at the tabernacle door: and all the people rose up and worshipped, every man in his tent door.

Again, on the surface it appears that the people had repented. When they saw the cloud they worshipped. But did you notice where they worshiped from? They never left their houses. They saw that Moses would go into the presence of God. They must have seen Joshua go in as well. But they never once attempted to get any closer to God than from the comfort of their own homes. But Joshua had the right idea.

Exodus 33:11
*And the LORD spake unto Moses face to face, as a man
speaketh unto his friend. And he turned again into the
camp: but his servant Joshua, the son of Nun, a young
man, departed not out of the tabernacle.*

1 Corinthians 10:1-5 tells us that their worship was with
their mouths but their hearts were far from God.

1ˢᵗ Corinthians 10:1-5
*Moreover, brethren, I would not that ye should be
ignorant, how that all our fathers were under the cloud,
and all passed through the sea; 10:2 And were all
baptized unto Moses in the cloud and in the sea; 10:3 And
did all eat the same spiritual meat; 10:4 And did all drink
the same spiritual drink: for they drank of that spiritual
Rock that followed them: and that Rock was Christ. 10:5
But with many of them God was not well pleased: for they
were overthrown in the wilderness.*

Moses knew that the very presence of God in their camp
served a purpose.

First, it was to reveal God to the Jews.
Second, it was to be a sign to all the other nations that God
was with them.

Exodus 33:15-16
*And he said unto him, If thy presence go not with me, carry
us not up hence. 33:16 For wherein shall it be known here
that I and thy people have found grace in thy sight? is it
not in that thou goest with us? so shall we be separated, I
and thy people, from all the people that are upon the face
of the earth.*

You see, there must be something that separates a
Christian from the rest of the world. What is it? The
presence of God in the church is seen by the love we have
for one another.

John 13:35
*By this shall all men know that ye are my disciples, if ye
have love one to another.*

The presence is seen by the life you live.

Psalm 1:1-3
*Blessed is the man that walketh not in the counsel of the
ungodly, nor standeth in the way of sinners, nor sitteth in
the seat of the scornful. 1:2 But his delight is in the law of
the LORD; and in his law doth he meditate day and night.
1:3 And he shall be like a tree planted by the rivers of
water, that bringeth forth his fruit in his season; his leaf
also shall not wither; and whatsoever he doeth shall
prosper.*

God's presence is seen by the signs and wonders that occur
through those who believe.

Mark 16:20
*And they went forth, and preached every where, the Lord
working with them, and confirming the word with signs
following.*

Signs and wonders accompanied what? The Word of God
that was preached by the disciples!

Exodus 33:17
And the LORD said unto Moses, I will do this thing also

that thou hast spoken: for thou hast found grace in my sight, and I know thee by name.

3. It is a must: That we rest in God's glory

Moses now has everything set in place for him to continue the work that he was called to do. He has the calling and he has the presence. He is ready to go! But he asks for one more thing.

Exodus 33:18
And he said, I beseech thee, show me thy glory.

You know, I feel like I had an advantage over some people when I came to know the Lord. I had a family who witnessed and prayed for me before I was saved. And I immediately developed a hunger for more of God after I was saved. I knew God's presence was real through the evidence of the change in my inner man. But, I began to want more.

I started seeking His glory. I knew it was for the asking. I knew if I wanted more and that God would somehow satisfy that. It was even to the point that in our traditional church denomination I could not wait for the doors to open, because I knew that God was somehow going to reveal Himself to me in a new and refreshing way. I did not know how. I did not know what to expect. I just knew… and praise God that is exactly what happened.

Exodus 33:19
And he said, I will make all my goodness pass before thee, and I will proclaim the name of the LORD before thee; and will be gracious to whom I will be gracious, and will show

mercy on whom I will show mercy.

Exodus 33:21
And the LORD said, Behold, there is a place by me, and thou shalt stand upon a rock:

Three things to see here;

1) For those who seek that deeper relationship with the Lord He will reveal Himself in a new way.

Jeremiah 33:3
Call unto me, and I will answer thee, and shew thee great and mighty things, which thou knowest not.

2) He will reveal His nature (His name) to you in a new way.

Exodus 6:3-6
And Moses said, I will now turn aside, and see this great sight, why the bush is not burnt. 3:4 And when the LORD saw that he turned aside to see, God called unto him out of the midst of the bush, and said, Moses, Moses. And he said, Here am I. 3:5 And he said, Draw not nigh hither: put off thy shoes from off thy feet, for the place whereon thou standest is holy ground. 3:6 Moreover he said, I am the God of thy father, the God of Abraham, the God of Isaac, and the God of Jacob. And Moses hid his face; for he was afraid to look upon God.

Today we know what that Name is.

1st Corinthians 10:4
And did all drink the same spiritual drink: for they drank

of that spiritual Rock that followed them: and that Rock was Christ.

3) He has set a place for you to stand in His presence.

1st Corinthians 10:1-4
Moreover, brethren, I would not that ye should be ignorant, how that all our fathers were under the cloud, and all passed through the sea; 10:2 And were all baptized unto Moses in the cloud and in the sea; 10:3 And did all eat the same spiritual meat; 10:4 And did all drink the same spiritual drink: for they drank of that spiritual Rock that followed them: and that Rock was Christ.

In order for us to follow God's presence, we must see the visible presence of God in us. We were changed at our salvation and baptism (sanctification/consecration). We were empowered with the baptism in the Holy Spirit. His presence is at work in our lives. We are in a constant state of change – from glory to glory.

God's manifest presence now is filling the Temple.

Do you want to see the presence of God?
Then remember the call He has placed on your life.

Do you want to sense His presence and power in your life? Look no further than His word and all the promises that are yours.

Do you want to see His glory? His glory now rests in the Holy Spirit who dwells in each of you and manifests Himself in power through you.

Are we willing to be like Moses?

Are we willing to say to the Lord, "I will go wherever You go and say whatever You say"?

Are we willing to be like that next generation of Israelites who consecrated themselves, and then stood in the river because that is where God's presence was?

His presence, through the Holy Spirit, will take you deeper with God.

Romans 8:14
For as many as are led by the Spirit of God, they are the sons of God.

Follow His Presence.

Chapter 5

Trust in His Word

Hebrews 4:12-13

If you want God's miracles you have to trust His Word.

Hebrews 4:12-13
For the word of God is quick, and powerful, and sharper than any two-edged sword, piercing even to the dividing asunder of soul and spirit, and of the joints and marrow, and is a discerner of the thoughts and intents of the heart. 4:13 Neither is there any creature that is not manifest in his sight: but all things are naked and opened unto the eyes of him with whom we have to do.

Let's start this chapter with a two-part question.

First, do you have anyone in your life that you can absolutely trust all the time? I mean, that without any doubt, you know that person will be there for you in every circumstance to stand behind you. You know that person has your back at all times. I would hope that most of us has a person like that in our lives.

Now, the second part… If you have someone like that in your life, and I hope you do, are you willing to actually come to the place where you are willing to put that trust into action? Not just saying you trust but actively trusting!

How many of you remember your first time on an airplane? Tell me the truth; were you a little apprehensive about the ability of a thing so huge flying through the air? There is a story that goes like this:

Uncle Oscar was apprehensive about his first airplane ride. His friends, eager to hear how it went, asked if he enjoyed the flight.

"Well," commented Uncle Oscar, "it wasn't as bad as I thought it might be, but I'll tell you this. I never did put all my weight down!" Too funny!

Many Christians can relate to Uncle Oscar in their relationship with God. They are apprehensive when they first get on. They see that it works just fine, but they never put their full trust in Him. That creates a real dilemma.

First, how can you ever come to the place of complete trust unless you make a conscious decision to do so?

Second, if you haven't placed all your trust in Him is it really trust?

We have the ability to know God as He truly deserves and desires to be known. We have a holy book that is God's perfect revelation of Himself to mankind. It is His word! And since it is His word and not our rendition of His word we can trust it.

2 Peter 1:20-21
Knowing this first, that no prophecy of the scripture is of any private interpretation. 1:21 For the prophecy came not in old time by the will of man: but holy men of God spake as they were moved by the Holy Ghost.

So, if this book that we hold so dear, is what it claims to be – God's Word – then we must realize that, in order to receive a miracle from God, one of the steps we must take is to trust this word completely and without doubting.

This will require us realizing some things.

<u>1ˢᵗ God's Word is living</u>

Hebrews 4:12
For the word of God is quick,

This word quick means, 'living'. "For the word of God is living…" The Greek word translated "word" here is "logos". Logos refers to God's written word and the "rhema" is God's spoken word. That is somewhat accurate but it goes deeper than that.

'Logos' refers to God's disclosure or revelation of Himself to the world. It comes from the root word 'lego' which means, 'to lay forth, or an individual expression or to break silence'. If you look at the 'logos' in that way we can see three things:

1) The word lays forth a foundation – God spoke the world and all of creation into existence with what? His word!
In Genesis 1:3, 6, 9, 11, 20, 24 before each creative act we read, "and God said…"

2) God's word is an individual expression of His being.

John 1:1
In the beginning was the Word, and the Word was with God, and the Word was God.

The very nature of God was revealed through the person Jesus Christ.

Hebrews 1:3
Who being the brightness of his glory, and the express

image of his person, and upholding all things by the word of his power, when he had by himself purged our sins, sat down on the right hand of the Majesty on high:

Here we see God's glory expressed in the image of Christ Jesus, sustaining all things by His powerful word who took away our sin and is set down in power in His rightful place on high.

3) The word of God breaks the silence. Since the fall of man, there has been a great disconnect between heaven and earth. It is not that God was silent in that He did not speak to men, but it has become increasingly difficult for men to hear God's voice. But through the work of the cross, and, because of His written word, the silence is broken. We can understand the very nature of God by looking at Jesus and by seeing His nature revealed through the scriptures. Now, that tells us what the word of God is and that should be enough to make you trust His word.

But let us go a step further.

What is God's word doing?

First, it is a living word. One of the great arguments to be brought against the Bible is exemplified in this statement from an article written by a Muslim apologist, Ahmed Deedat,

"Yes, the Bible is human, though some, out of zeal which is not according to knowledge, have denied this. Those books have passed through the minds of men, are written in the language of men, were penned by the hands of men, and bear in their style the characteristics of men."

In this same article Deedat quotes so-called "Christian leaders" as saying that they themselves do not believe the Bible to be the word of God. But our passage and the internal evidence of the Bible itself dictates that we profess otherwise.

The word of God is living. It is not some ancient manuscript that has outlived its usefulness. It is timeless. Jesus said in Matthew 24:35, "Heaven and earth will pass away, but my words will never pass away". There is a great theological chasm that is cast between Bible believers and liberal theologians. We believe that the Bible is God's word. They believe that it contains God's word but is not totally God's word. One of the evidences that we have is the evidence of changed lives.
(A side note here; I read on Friday that an Episcopal Bishop has proclaimed that individual salvation is a heresy. Salvation can only come through the church and the church alone and for anyone to believe that an individual can be saved by his repentance and confession makes him a heretic.)

Realize, dear friend, that the church cannot change anyone. A pastor or a priest cannot pronounce you saved. Salvation is an inward change that effects the outward. God has given us the example. He has given us the formula. Repent, be baptized for the remission of sin, and then you will be clean enough to receive the gift of the Holy Ghost. This is the Word of God.

I don't know what bible this priest has been reading. When I read the Bible, it changes me. I am saved by grace through faith, and the word is still changing me because it is active. The truth of the word is to be taken literally unless it is declared within itself to be symbolic. That is why there is such a vast difference in understanding of the Word. Many try to make too much of the Bible an allegory instead of taking the words at face value.

The word is not only living, it is active.

Isaiah 55:10-11
For as the rain cometh down, and the snow from heaven, and returneth not thither, but watereth the earth, and maketh it bring forth and bud, that it may give seed to the sower, and bread to the eater: 55:11 So shall my word be that goeth forth out of my mouth: it shall not return unto me void, but it shall accomplish that which I please, and it shall prosper in the thing whereto I sent it.

But the truth of the Word is hidden from unbelievers.

2 Corinthians 4:1-4
Therefore seeing we have this ministry, as we have received mercy, we faint not;
 4:2 But have renounced the hidden things of dishonesty, not walking in craftiness, nor handling the word of God deceitfully; but by manifestation of the truth commending ourselves to every man's conscience in the sight of God. 4:3 But if our gospel be hid, it is hid to them that are lost: 4:4 In whom the god of this world hath blinded the minds of them which believe not, lest the light of the glorious gospel of Christ, who is the image of God, should shine unto them.

If you want to take a step toward receiving God's promises you must come to the place where you can confess that:

It is the Word of God,
It is a living word,
It is as active now as it has ever been.

2. God's Word is penetrating

Hebrews 4:12
For the word of God is quick, and powerful, and sharper than any two-edged sword, piercing even to the dividing asunder of soul and spirit, and of the joints and marrow, and is a discerner of the thoughts and intents of the heart.

'For the word of God is living and active. Sharper than any double-edged sword'. It penetrates… Though the enemy of your soul has blinded the minds of unbelievers we must understand that the word is intended to touch the hearts of man. Yes, it is true that some may come to salvation by understanding the gospel first, but salvation does not come until the word of God takes root in the heart where the seed is planted.

It is interesting that in Ephesians 6 Paul tells us that the sword of the Spirit is the word of God. This sword is sharp. The word translated "sharper" refers to a blade that is able to do its work with a single stroke. It does not need to keep hacking away. But, since it is a double-edged sword it can protect and attack from either side, regardless of the angle of attack.

As a Christian you do not need any other weapon. How deeply does the word go into a man? What activity takes place when the word of God is proclaimed? '…it penetrates even to dividing soul and spirit, joints and marrow; it judges the thoughts and attitudes of the heart'.

When we do evangelism, we present the gospel in a way that bypasses the mind, the place of argument, and goes straight to the heart or conscience. The word works that way for salvation but it also works that way for receiving all God's promises. You see, until you can bypass the mind, the place of argument, where the spiritual battles take place, and allow the word to go directly to the heart or spirit man, you cannot have the faith to receive His miracles in your life.

I have seen so many through the years that have a head knowledge. They have been to some of the finest universities but they have no heart knowledge. I am not discrediting colleges or schools. I think they are great, but until the Gospel truly touches you, you will never see the miracle working power of God that you are seeking for. Faith never stems from the soul, or the mind or emotions, but from the spirit or heart.

2 Corinthians 10:4-5
(For the weapons of our warfare are not carnal, but mighty through God to the pulling down of strong holds;) 10:5 Casting down imaginations, and every high thing that exalteth itself against the knowledge of God, and bringing into captivity every thought to the obedience of Christ;

We do not allow our thoughts to steal the victory away from us. God's word divides soul and spirit. It is sharp enough to separate the joints and the marrow – like a surgeon's scalpel – and it judges the thoughts and the attitudes of the heart or your motives. Look at what James says about having the right motives in receiving the work of God in your life.

James 4:1-3
From whence come wars and fightings among you? come they not hence, even of your lusts that war in your members? 4:2 Ye lust, and have not: ye kill, and desire to have, and cannot obtain: ye fight and war, yet ye have not, because ye ask not. 4:3 Ye ask, and receive not, because ye ask amiss, that ye may consume it upon your lusts.

There are three things James talks about here concerning motives:

1). Your relationships with other Christians are not where they should be. Your desires control you instead of your relationship with the Lord.

2) You allow doubt to enter your mind and control your life so that you don't even bother asking God for the very things you need.

3) You want what you want when you want it. Your prayer is always about you and never about God. You will not receive anything that way. But the word, when applied to the heart, will change that if you let it.

3. God's Word is revealing

Hebrews 4:13
Neither is there any creature that is not manifest in his sight: but all things are naked and opened unto the eyes of him with whom we have to do.

I want to take a closer look at this one verse.

First of all,

Nothing in all creation is hidden from God's sight.

Everything is uncovered and laid bare… That pretty much covers everything doesn't it?

Nothing in all creation is hidden from God's sight.

Everything has been created. The creator knows everything about His creation. As a boy I used to help my dad build houses. My dad was a carpenter and a farmer. My dad took great care in every house he built. He built it as if he was going to live there himself. But when the house was finished my dad would go through and point out little imperfections. He knew every part of every house. How? He created it. He built it.

Since we are God's creation, we cannot hide anything from Him. He knows your thoughts, but what is more important is that He knows your heart. Everything is uncovered and laid bare… Now, I do not want your train of thought to stop there. I want you to go on to the rest of the verse.

Everything is uncovered and laid bare before the eyes of him to whom we must give account.

We are accountable to God for all things in our lives.

1) We are accountable for our own salvation.

Psalm 37:39
But the salvation of the righteous is of the LORD: he is their strength in the time of trouble.

Every human being from Adam to the last people standing when all things are created anew will have to give an account to God for their spiritual status. God has given all men the opportunity to be saved, and at the end all who refused will give an account.

2) The word of God judges sin in the lives of all people. That is the whole purpose of the commandments – to show people their sin and their need for a Savior.

3) Even believers will be judged for their actions and their failings. This is not to determine heaven of hell but their rewards in heaven. But, I want to go beyond salvation. Since we are talking about trusting God's word in order to receive a miracle in our lives, one of the things God will ask you is, "Why didn't you receive the promises I had in store for you while you were on the earth?"

Luke 18:8
.... Nevertheless when the Son of man cometh, shall he find faith on the earth?

Many have taught this to mean, 'when Jesus returns, will there be saving faith on the earth'. But we know that when Jesus comes back in the clouds He is coming for His bride, the church. So there has to be faith, right? I take this to mean that, even among the saved, 'will Jesus find full, complete trust in His word'. He is asking, "When I come back will my word still be living and active in the church?"

Psalm 119:57-58
Thou art my portion, O LORD: I have said that I would keep thy words. 119:58 I intreated thy favour with my

whole heart: be merciful unto me according to thy word.

We can only trust God's word when we have come to the place in our lives where we are willing to:

1) consecrate ourselves – be set aside through salvation for God's purpose.
2) stand in the river of the Holy Spirit and let Him fill you to overflowing,
3) Follow God's presence; go where He goes and do what He does and say what He says.
4) Trust God's word. See, if the word of God were some contrived manuscript intended to make people spiritual robots it would be no different than Hitler's Mein Kampf or Mao Tse – Tung's little red book. But this book is different. It is spiritual and not philosophical. It is life changing.

Proverbs 30:5-6
Every word of God is pure: he is a shield unto them that put their trust in him. 30:6 Add thou not unto his words, lest he reprove thee, and thou be found a liar.

The problem with our ability to trust God's word is that we too often focus on what the word says we cannot do instead of all the wonderful things that are available to us right here and right now.

Author Tim Hansel writes,
"One day, while my son Zac and I were out in the country, climbing around in some cliffs, I heard a voice from above me yell, "Hey Dad! Catch me!" I turned around to see Zac joyfully jumping off a rock straight at me. He had jumped and then yelled "Hey Dad!" I became an instant circus act,

catching him. We both fell to the ground. For a moment after I caught him I could hardly talk.

When I found my voice again I gasped in exasperation: "Zac! Can you give me one good reason why you did that???"

He responded with remarkable calmness: "Sure...because you're my Dad." His whole assurance was based in the fact that his father was trustworthy. He could live life to the hilt because I could be trusted. Isn't this even more true for a Christian?"

Tim Hansel, Holy Sweat, 1987, Word Books Publisher, pp. 46-47.

God is asking you today, "Will you just believe my word? I have so many wonderful things in store for you before you even get to heaven. And if you will just accept them by faith you will see My name glorified in all the earth."

Chapter 6

Step out on Faith

Mark 5:21-43

In order to get a miracle from God you have to go to Jesus with your need.

Mark 5:21-43
And when Jesus was passed over again by ship unto the other side, much people gathered unto him: and he was nigh unto the sea. 5:22 And, behold, there cometh one of the rulers of the synagogue, Jairus by name; and when he saw him, he fell at his feet, 5:23 And besought him greatly, saying, My little daughter lieth at the point of death: I pray thee, come and lay thy hands on her, that she may be healed; and she shall live. 5:24 And Jesus went with him; and much people followed him, and thronged him. 5:25 And a certain woman, which had an issue of blood twelve years, 5:26 And had suffered many things of many physicians, and had spent all that she had, and was nothing bettered, but rather grew worse, 5:27 When she had heard of Jesus, came in the press behind, and touched his garment. 5:28 For she said, If I may touch but his clothes, I shall be whole. 5:29 And straightway the fountain of her blood was dried up; and she felt in her body that she was healed of that plague. 5:30 And Jesus, immediately knowing in himself that virtue had gone out of him, turned him about in the press, and said, Who touched my clothes? 5:31 And his disciples said unto him, Thou seest the multitude thronging thee, and sayest thou, Who touched me? 5:32 And he looked round about to see her that had done this thing. 5:33 But the woman fearing and trembling, knowing what was done in her, came and fell down before him, and told him all the truth. 5:34 And he said unto her, Daughter, thy faith hath made thee whole; go in peace, and be whole of thy plague.

5:35 While he yet spake, there came from the ruler of the synagogue's house certain which said, Thy daughter is dead: why troublest thou the Master any further? 5:36 As soon as Jesus heard the word that was spoken, he saith unto the ruler of the synagogue, Be not afraid, only believe. 5:37 And he suffered no man to follow him, save Peter, and James, and John the brother of James. 5:38 And he cometh to the house of the ruler of the synagogue, and seeth the tumult, and them that wept and wailed greatly. 5:39 And when he was come in, he saith unto them, Why make ye this ado, and weep? the damsel is not dead, but sleepeth. 5:40 And they laughed him to scorn. But when he had put them all out, he taketh the father and the mother of the damsel, and them that were with him, and entereth in where the damsel was lying. 5:41 And he took the damsel by the hand, and said unto her, Talitha cumi; which is, being interpreted, Damsel, I say unto thee, arise. 5:42 And straightway the damsel arose, and walked; for she was of the age of twelve years. And they were astonished with a great astonishment. 5:43 And he charged them straitly that no man should know it; and commanded that something should be given her to eat.

Okay, here are the facts. We have been going step by step toward receiving a miracle in our lives. Everyone needs a miracle. If you are reading this book right now and somehow have convinced yourself that you do not need anything from God right now I ask you to search your heart a little deeper and find that need that you never considered before. The first four steps that we have discussed all concern a work of God and your response to that work.

1. Consecrate Yourself – God's offer of salvation through Jesus Christ and your acceptance of that work, repenting of your sins, being baptized in Jesus' name for the remission of your sins.

2. Stand in the River – Jesus' promise to baptize believers in the Holy Spirit and your willingness to ask for and receive power.

3. Follow God's presence — Seek God's will for your life and then follow the instructions He gives you.

4. Trust God's word — God has given us His word and it is up to us to believe that this holy book is exactly what it says it is – the Holy Spirit inspired word of God.

Now we move into a little different area. We move from what God has done in order for us to receive to what we must do in order to receive that miracle we are looking for. And it requires faith on our part. We are told that we must step out in faith in order to receive the things that make no sense to us. But we have spent the last five chapters explaining that God intends for you to have more than what you are currently experiencing with Him. He wants you to have a miracle.

Before we go any further, I want you to understand what a miracle is. Many people will look at a newborn baby and say that it is a miracle. Well, as callous as it might seem, babies are not miracles. Babies are something that God has ordained to happen according to the natural laws that He has set in place.

Real miracles are things that happen outside the natural laws that God has established. For instance – God has set the law of gravity into operation. If you stepped off the edge of a roof, the natural law of gravity would go into effect and adverse consequences would follow. However, if you stepped off the edge of a roof and nothing happened – you just floated in mid-air – that would be a miracle.

Those are the types of events that God has planned for your life. He wants you to receive what you need so that the only possible explanation would be that God worked a miracle.

I want to look at a comparison of two different people who encountered a miracle from Jesus.

How can you receive your miracle?

1st You will need to recognize your need.

I want you to see, first of all, that Jesus' popularity had increased greatly over the course of His ministry.

Mark 5:21-22
And when Jesus was passed over again by ship unto the other side, much people gathered unto him: and he was nigh unto the sea. 5:22 And, behold, there cometh one of the rulers of the synagogue, Jairus by name; and when he saw him, he fell at his feet,

As we begin the story, we see Jairus, one of the synagogue rulers, coming to Jesus with a request. Jairus was not a priest, but a layman who would be in charge of the order of the service in the synagogue. He would have been someone who was held in high esteem by others. He worshiped the One true God. But in his limited understanding of the nature of God, an understanding that would have been tainted by the additions to the scriptures and the traditions of the Pharisees and others, he really did not have a grasp on what God wanted to do for him.

It is interesting that this Jew, a ruler of the synagogue, would be coming to the one that the Jewish leaders had already rejected because of his anti-religion activities. But he had a need and he turned to Jesus to have that need met.

Next, I want you to look at the story that is inserted in the middle of the story of Jairus. A large crowd followed and pressed around him.

Mark 5:25-26
And a certain woman, which had an issue of blood twelve years, 5:26 And had suffered many things of many physicians, and had spent all that she had, and was nothing bettered, but rather grew worse,
Here is a woman who had suffered at the hands of doctors for twelve years.

We don't have any idea what might have caused her problem. All we know is that the doctors drained her finances and put her through painful treatments and it didn't help. She just got worse. I suppose that she was just ready for it all to come to a merciful end.

The Jewish law would, because of her impurity:
have her husband divorce her,
her friends disown her,
her synagogue excommunicate her, and

society ostracize her;
all because of her uncleanness, something that was out of
her control.

Then something in her life changed.

Mark 5:27
When she had heard of Jesus…

We do not know what she heard, but I do know this, faith
comes by hearing. My guess would be that she heard about
this itinerant preacher going around the countryside casting
out demons, confronting the religious leaders, and healing
people, making the cripple to walk and the blind to see. Up
to this point Jesus had never been an option for her. She
had tried in her own efforts to take care of the problem.

What is it that keeps people from recognizing their needs?
Is it because society has always pushed us toward the idea
of individualism?
Stand up for yourself.
Be a man!
Take the bull by the horns.
Asking for help is a sign of weakness.

A poll sheds light on a paradox of increased religiosity and
decreased morality, according to sociologist Robert Bellah.

His conclusion: "81 percent of the American people say an
individual should arrive at his or her own religious belief
independent of any church or synagogue."

Thus the key to the paradox is that those who claim to be Christians are arriving at faith on their own terms -- terms that make no demands on behavior.

A woman named Sheila, interviewed for Bellah's Habits of the Heart, embodies this attitude: "I believe in God," she said. "I can't remember the last time I went to church. But my faith has carried me a long way. It is 'Sheila-ism.' Just my own little voice." I'll do it my way.

Charles Colson, Against the Night, p. 98

Proverbs 14:12
There is a way which seemeth right unto a man, but the end thereof are the ways of death.

1st Peter 5:7 says it very plainly
Casting all your care upon him; for he careth for you.

2nd **Present your need to Jesus.**

As a Christian, it is not enough to just recognize your need. You must bring it to Jesus.

Mark 5:22-23
And, behold, there cometh one of the rulers of the synagogue, Jairus by name; and when he saw him, he fell at his feet, 5:23 And besought him greatly, saying, My little daughter lieth at the point of death: I pray thee, come and lay thy hands on her, that she may be healed; and she shall live.

Jairus must have seen Jesus at work before. It is likely that as Jesus went around Galilee and preached in the synagogues and healed on the Sabbath, one of those episodes took place in the synagogue where Jairus was the ruler.

Mark 3:1-6 tells such a story.
And he entered again into the synagogue; and there was a man there which had a withered hand. 3:2 And they watched him, whether he would heal him on the sabbath day; that they might accuse him. 3:3 And he saith unto the man which had the withered hand, Stand forth. 3:4 And he saith unto them, Is it lawful to do good on the sabbath days, or to do evil? to save life, or to kill? But they held their peace. 3:5 And when he had looked round about on them with anger, being grieved for the hardness of their hearts, he saith unto the man, Stretch forth thine hand. And he stretched it out: and his hand was restored whole as the other. 3:6 And the Pharisees went forth, and straightway took counsel with the Herodians against him, how they might destroy him.

From seeing Jesus at work before Jairus may have had a preconceived notion as to how Jesus would heal. I want you to notice this. Jairus came to Jesus face to face and then fell on his knees before Him. When the crowd would have seen him coming they would have stepped aside because of his position, and let him pass through. The last thing they expected would be for a leader of the synagogue to fall on his knees before the One who was bringing an end to their traditions.

Even though we know that Jesus did not have to be present in order for healing to take place, Jesus honored his request because it was asked in faith.

Mark 5:24
And Jesus went with him

Now turn your thoughts back to the woman in the story. Here is a different approach.

Mark 5:27-28
When she had heard of Jesus, came in the press behind, and touched his garment. 5:28 For she said, If I may touch but his clothes, I shall be whole.

Luke's version of this story tells us that the crowd had pressed in so closely to Jesus that He was close to being crushed. This woman, in her desperation does two wise things:

1) She approaches Jesus from behind. Had she attempted to get to Him from the front she would have been prevented from coming to Him. One, because women never approached men in public without a husband present, and two, she would have been recognized as an unclean woman and cast aside.

2) She makes up her mind that nothing is going to keep her from getting to Jesus. Now, remember, we are talking about stepping out in faith to receive a miracle. In order for you to step out in faith you must believe that there is a miracle waiting for you, then you need to get in the presence of the miracle worker.

3rd You need get hold of Jesus

Let us stay with the woman for a few minutes. Why was
there such a great crowd that was following Jesus? It was
because of the message He preached and the miracles He
had done. The people who were around Jesus had seen
Him heal before and were expecting it to happen again.
Look what it says happened when the woman finally got to
Jesus.

She was in the middle of a great crowd that was expecting,
but it was something on her part that had brought her
healing. Let us continue,

*gone out of him, turned him about in the press, and said,
Who touched my clothes? 5:31 And his disciples said unto
him, Thou seest the multitude thronging thee, and sayest
thou, Who touched me? 5:32 And he looked round about
to see her that had done this thing. 5:33 But the woman
fearing and trembling, knowing what was done in her,
came and fell down before him, and told him all the truth*

This woman had done nothing to be ashamed of. She was
not being chastised by Jesus for her act of faith. He wanted
to make personal contact with her so she could know that it
was not some superstitious belief that had healed her but
her encounter with the supernatural healer. Just a quick
addition to this; Jesus never healed except for the purpose
of bringing glory to the Father.

John 14:13-14
*And whatsoever ye shall ask in my name, that will I do,
that the Father may be glorified in the Son. 14:14 If ye
shall ask any thing in my name, I will do it. 14:15 If ye
love me, keep my commandments.*

Jesus made sure that everyone understood what had
happened.

Mark 5: 34
*And he said unto her, Daughter, thy faith hath made thee
whole; go in peace, and be whole of thy plague.*

Now we go back to the other story.

While the rejoicing was taking place in the middle of the
crowd, sad news comes.

Mark 5:35
While he yet spake, there came from the ruler of the synagogue's house certain which said, Thy daughter is dead: why troublest thou the Master any further?

Did you ever wonder why these two stories were linked together like this?

First of all, it is the way it happened.
Secondly, God knew that Jairus would need a faith booster. He was preparing him for what was about to happen.

Mark 5:36
As soon as Jesus heard the word that was spoken, he saith unto the ruler of the synagogue, Be not afraid, only believe.

I want you to see what happens next. Jesus separates Himself from the crowd. I find this very interesting. This large gathering had just witnessed a miraculous healing where twelve years of doctor's treatments had failed. Wouldn't you think that this crowd would be so pumped that it would be to Jesus' advantage to take a crowd of faith along with Him? But, no. This is a private matter. A man had just lost his daughter. The crowd did not need to see this. Jesus' compassion for his loss is rising up in him.

Mark 5:37
And he suffered no man to follow him, save Peter, and James, and John the brother of James.

Jesus took His "inner circle" of friends with Him. The reason He left the crowd behind becomes evident in the next passage.

Mark 5:38
And he cometh to the house of the ruler of the synagogue, and seeth the tumult, and them that wept and wailed greatly.

Matthew 9:23
And when Jesus came into the ruler's house, and saw the minstrels and the people making a noise,

There were flute players there also. It looks like funeral preparations were already in place. The professional mourners were there as well as the musicians. The little girl was dead and that was a fact.

Mark 5:39-40
And when he was come in, he saith unto them, Why make ye this ado, and weep? the damsel is not dead, but sleepeth. 5:40 And they laughed him to scorn. But when he had put them all out, he taketh the father and the mother of the damsel, and them that were with him, and entereth in where the damsel was lying.

Jesus did not mean that she was literally asleep. He meant that this was just a temporary state. He had his mind set on one thing – the miracle that was about to take place and nothing could keep Him from it. After he put them all out, he took the child's father and mother and the disciples who were with him, and went in where the child was.

Mark 5:41-42
And he took the damsel by the hand, and said unto her, Talitha cumi; which is, being interpreted, Damsel, I say unto thee, arise. 5:42 And straightway the damsel arose, and walked; for she was of the age of twelve years. And they were astonished with a great astonishment.

Why do we consider one supernatural work of God to be more incredible than another? Why is raising the dead more miraculous than healing a woman? Why do we look at miracles in degrees rather than what they are – the supernatural work of God?

I want to end with verse 43,

Mark 5:43
And he charged them straitly that no man should know it; and commanded that something should be given her to eat.

In the first story Jesus healed the woman out in the open in front of a great crowd of people. There was no way it could be kept a secret. But the second miracle was done in private and Jesus told them not to tell anyone. Why? It is because of the difference in the crowd? The first crowd, the common people, was attracted to Jesus because of the miracle. The second crowd would most likely have been the "religious crowd" who were already convinced that Jesus had come to oppose their Law and traditions.

His desire for the first crowd was to draw them to His words by the miracle. His desire for the second crowd was to come to Him by faith that was established from their own scriptures. Those very scriptures attested to who Jesus was. The Jews didn't need miracles. They needed Jesus.

Jesus wants you to have the miracle, or miracles, that you need in your life.

Have you taken all the necessary previous steps to receive your miracle?

Now is the time to step out in faith and come to Jesus with your need.
It doesn't matter who you are.
It doesn't matter what your need is.
All that matters is that you are willing to come to Jesus and present your needs to Him personally, with faith, and then watch Him work.

Are you desperate enough to push through the crowd? It does not matter whether you are touching Jesus in a crowded church service or in the privacy of your prayer closet. Jesus wants you to have your miracle.

Step out in faith and receive your miracle today.

Chapter 7

Going Over into the Supernatural

Philippians 3:12-20

Once you have experienced God's miracles in your life there is no reason for you not to continue to walk in the spirit realm on a regular basis.

Philippians 3:12-20
Not as though I had already attained, either were already perfect: but I follow after, if that I may apprehend that for which also I am apprehended of Christ Jesus. 3:13 Brethren, I count not myself to have apprehended: but this one thing I do, forgetting those things which are behind, and reaching forth unto those things which are before, 3:14 I press toward the mark for the prize of the high calling of God in Christ Jesus. 3:15 Let us therefore, as many as be perfect, be thus minded: and if in any thing ye be otherwise minded, God shall reveal even this unto you. 3:16 Nevertheless, whereto we have already attained, let us walk by the same rule, let us mind the same thing. 3:17 Brethren, be followers together of me, and mark them which walk so as ye have us for an ensample. 3:18 (For many walk, of whom I have told you often, and now tell you even weeping, that they are the enemies of the cross of Christ: 3:19 Whose end is destruction, whose God is their belly, and whose glory is in their shame, who mind earthly things.) 3:20 For our conversation is in heaven; from whence also we look for the Saviour, the Lord Jesus Christ:

So far, we have gone from accepting the things that God has promised and stepping out in faith to receive them, to crossing over into the spirit realm in order to stay connected to what the Holy Spirit wants for your life. And that is where I want to take you. To step out in faith and receive the things of God in your life is one thing, but to cross over into the spirit realm and continue to walk in the Spirit is something more.

In ancient Greece the Olympic games had one race that was different than all the others. In this race it wasn't the one who finished first who won. It was the one who finished with his torch still lit.

That is God's desire for the church today – to finish the race with the torch of faith still blazing, so that we may continue to walk in the Spirit and in all the promises that our God has given us. How can we do that? How can we make that happen?

1st You have to cross over to what is yours.

You have taken that all important first step into the supernatural. You are in agreement with the scriptures about what God wants to do in your life. As a matter of fact, you understand that in God's time it is already done.

He is not going to do anything more to save, heal, provide for, or bless you than what He has already done. It was all accomplished at the cross.

Yet Paul says,

Philippians 3:12
Not as though I had already attained, either were already perfect:

Maybe there is something that you have been asking God for in your life for some time and yet you have not received it. It does not mean that it has not happened yet.

In truth, it already has happened in the spirit realm and now God is waiting to pour it out into your natural man or your physical body.

Mark 11:22-24
And Jesus answering saith unto them, Have faith in God. 11:23 For verily I say unto you, That whosoever shall say unto this mountain, Be thou removed, and be thou cast into the sea; and shall not doubt in his heart, but shall believe that those things which he saith shall come to pass; he shall have whatsoever he saith. 11:24 Therefore I say unto you, What things soever ye desire, when ye pray, believe that ye receive them, and ye shall have them.

You may not see the physical results of it yet but it is there and it is yours nonetheless. How can you do that? I mean, how can you have faith in something even though you have not seen the physical manifestation of it yet?

First of all, is that not what faith is?

Hebrews 11:1
Now faith is the substance of things hoped for, the evidence of things not seen.

Do you see heaven right now?
Does that make it any less real?
How do you know it is real?
By faith!

Second, faith begins in the heart or spirit of a man. The mind is the origin of doubt and not faith. If you have to wait until it makes sense you probably will never receive God's promise in your life.

Third, even though we do not see all the evidence right now, Paul tells us these things about heaven.

1) *In Ephesians 1:3*
Blessed be the God and Father of our Lord Jesus Christ, who hath blessed us with all spiritual blessings in heavenly places in Christ:

It doesn't take a degree in theology to understand what it is that God has blessed us with in the heavenly realms. The first thing He has blessed us with is eternal life. But it goes beyond that. When Jesus taught his disciples how to pray He said, "Your will be done on earth as it is in heaven." So the things that are experienced in heaven are intended to translate over into the natural for believers. Salvation is for eternal life but so many of God's other promises are intended for you on earth.

2) *1 Timothy 4:8*
...godliness is profitable unto all things, having promise of the life that now is, and of that which is to come.

So Paul can now say in Philippians 3:12,

Philippians 3:12
... but I follow after, if that I may apprehend that for which also I am apprehended of Christ Jesus.

How do you do that?
By accepting God's word by faith!

Did you ever stop to think why we don't receive as much from God as He would have us receive? Is it because we have convinced ourselves that it is just for eternity that Jesus died, rose again and ascended into heaven? My dear friend, there is so much more that Jesus has and wants for us, if we will just believe. Jesus told us that all things are possible to those that believe. (Mark 9:23)

Philippians 3:13-14
Brethren, I count not myself to have apprehended: but this one thing I do, forgetting those things which are behind, and reaching forth unto those things which are before, 3:14 I press toward the mark for the prize of the high calling of God in Christ Jesus.

You see, Paul understood that the promises were already his, and now he was willing to set aside a life that was under the control of the god of this world and to move into a new life of power and expectancy – a life in the Spirit that he could walk in continually. Paul had crossed over into the spirit realm.

2nd You have to Hold firm to what is yours.

Philippians 3:15
Let us therefore, as many as be perfect, be thus minded:

Back in Philippians 3:10 Paul said something that should really make you think:

Philippians 3:10
"That I may know him, and the power of his resurrection, and the fellowship of his sufferings, being made conformable unto his death;"

One of the meanings of the word translated "know" is "to be aware of". So Paul is saying, I want to be aware of the power of Jesus' resurrection in my life. I want to know that spiritual power is for me through the baptism in the Holy Spirit and through that power, which is the same power that was at work in the life of Jesus. I can hold on to the miracles that God wants to pour out into my life.

Ephesians 3:20-21
Now unto him that is able to do exceeding abundantly above all that we ask or think, according to the power that worketh in us, 3:21 Unto him be glory in the church by Christ Jesus throughout all ages, world without end. Amen.

Now go back to Philippians 3:15.

Philippians 3:15
Let us therefore, as many as be perfect, be thus minded: and if in any thing ye be otherwise minded, God shall reveal even this unto you.

Who is it that Paul is reminding that they should remember what God has in store for them? It is for the mature! And if on some point you think differently, that too God will make clear to you. God has not hidden His promises from you. He has not concealed His word from you but is continually revealing it to you by revelation through the Holy Spirit.

1 Corinthians 2:9-10
But as it is written, Eye hath not seen, nor ear heard, neither have entered into the heart of man, the things which God hath prepared for them that love him. 2:10 But

God hath revealed them unto us by his Spirit: for the Spirit searcheth all things, yea, the deep things of God.

At what point are we willing to cross over into what God has already done in the spirit realm and then hold on till we receive it in the natural? You know there are companies in the world that invest large sums of money in searching for lost treasure. They send ships with the latest equipment out trying to find sunken treasure. They have never seen it but they know that it is there somewhere so they keep looking and waiting till they see the proof of it.

Paul says that Christians should be the same way.

Philippians 3:16
Nevertheless, whereto we have already attained, let us walk by the same rule, let us mind the same thing.

Look at Hebrews 11:6.

Hebrews 11:6
But without faith it is impossible to please him: for he that cometh to God must believe that he is, and that he is a rewarder of them that diligently seek him.

In this verse I want you to focus on one word – believe. That word refers to: 'a constant faith, an ongoing relationship with God'. If this is so, then it must also be an ongoing faith in His word and all His promises with the signs and wonders and miracles that He has told us would follow all who believe. It is not a faith that comes and goes, but one that we can hold on to without wavering, because we know that the one who promised is true!

<u>**3rd Move forward to what has been claimed for you.**</u>

Philippians 3:17
Brethren, be followers together of me, and mark them
which walk so as ye have us for an ensample.

There are people in the church who have that kind of faith
– the kind where they are continually expecting God to do
something in their lives. For those who do not have that
kind of faith should keep your eyes on those who do and
use them as an encouragement for you to receive God's
promises and walk in the Spirit. Paul never stopped
expecting the power of God to be displayed in his life.

1 Corinthians 2:4
And my speech and my preaching was not with enticing
words of man's wisdom, but in demonstration of the Spirit
and of power:

Romans 15:17-19
I have therefore whereof I may glory through Jesus Christ
in those things which pertain to God. 15:18 For I will not
dare to speak of any of those things which Christ hath not
wrought by me, to make the Gentiles obedient, by word
and deed, 15:19 Through mighty signs and wonders, by the
power of the Spirit of God; so that from Jerusalem, and
round about unto Illyricum, I have fully preached the
gospel of Christ.

Paul continually moved forward in his life knowing that
God was always able to deliver him from the power of the
enemy.

Philippians 3:18-19
(For many walk, of whom I have told you often, and now
tell you even weeping, that they are the enemies of the
cross of Christ: 3:19 Whose end is destruction, whose
God is their belly, and whose glory is in their shame, who
mind earthly things.)

Do you see the compassion that Paul had for those who
were being blinded by the god of this age? But, he says,
regardless of how good those people appear to be (and
they are good Christian people) do not be influenced by
their understanding, or lack of understanding, concerning
what God wants to do in the church today.

The enemy is powerless over you. You have been given
authority over him and over all his demons, unless you
give them a foothold through unbelief.

Philippians 3:20-21
3:20 For our conversation is in heaven; from whence also
we look for the Saviour, the Lord Jesus Christ: 3:21 Who
shall change our vile body, that it may be fashioned like
unto his glorious body, according to the working whereby
he is able even to subdue all things unto himself.

Paul walked through his life on earth with eternity in mind.
Yet he fully understood that his faith and his understanding
of what God desired for his life had carried him through
and it was the faith for the here and now that would get
him through to eternity.

Do you understand that God has a miracle for you?

Do you understand that once you have received a miracle you have crossed over into the realm of the supernatural that begins in the spirit realm?

As we strive more and more to walk in the Spirit and live according to the Spirit, we will become conduits for spiritual activity among your friends and family. Once you begin to realize what God wants to do, then you will begin to see that He is not going to do anything on this earth outside of His church. You are the vessel that He has set apart to carry out the miraculous. It is you that He is waiting upon to cry out in prayer, step out in faith, and hold out in hope.

When Paul said, "No eye has seen, no ear has heard, no mind has conceived what God has prepared for those who love him", he was speaking of the natural man.

1 Corinthians 2:14
But the natural man receiveth not the things of the Spirit of God: for they are foolishness unto him: neither can he know them, because they are spiritually discerned.

But you are not that man. You have the Spirit of God, the overflowing of the Spirit, so that you can understand. You can walk in the Spirit realm and hold on to those miracles that are just waiting to manifest themselves in your life.

God is revealing His very nature, His desires for your life, His power and His love for you, to those who will seek His face and call out to Him.

Jeremiah 33:3
Call unto me, and I will answer thee, and shew thee great and mighty things, which thou knowest not.

God is calling us to the place where we can expect Him to move by His Spirit in our lives while we look to the eastern sky waiting for His return.

We have crossed over into the supernatural.

Open your hearts to the things God has promised you and hold tight; regardless how you feel, regardless what you see, hold to those promises that He has made to you.

Chapter 8

Standing Firm – Remembering Who Has Promised

Psalm 77:10-15

Now that you have done everything you need to do, stand firm in the word of God.

Psalm 77:10-15
And I said, This is my infirmity: but I will remember the years of the right hand of the most High. 77:11 I will remember the works of the LORD: surely I will remember thy wonders of old. 77:12 I will meditate also of all thy work, and talk of thy doings. 77:13 Thy way, O God, is in the sanctuary: who is so great a God as our God? 77:14 Thou art the God that doest wonders: thou hast declared thy strength among the people. 77:15 Thou hast with thine arm redeemed thy people, the sons of Jacob and Joseph. Selah.

As you have read this book I hope and pray that the Lord has taken you into a new level of receiving His miracles upon your life. I pray that you have found a new level of commitment and trust. As we move into this last chapter, I believe that this is just the start of your journey to greater miracles.

The same God who healed the sick in the Bible is still willing to do the same today. God still provides for needs now as much as He did from the beginning of time.

Jesus Christ is the same yesterday, today and forever. And now you can see the results if you will persevere and expect with no showdown of doubting.

Could it be that for so long God has been waiting for you more than you have been waiting for Him? He was waiting for you to:

1. Consecrate yourself and be set apart for His purpose…

2. Stand in the river to receive power from on high…

3. Follow God's presence by seeking His face and His will for your life…

4. Trust His word and believe every promise He has given you…

5. Step out in faith in order to receive what He has already done…

6. Cross over into the supernatural to walk in the spirit…

Finally, we know that God is calling us to one last step to receive the miracle you have been waiting for. That step is to stand firm in all the other steps until God moves in your life.

Psalm 5:1-3
Give ear to my words, O LORD, consider my meditation. 5:2 Hearken unto the voice of my cry, my King, and my God: for unto thee will I pray. 5:3 My voice shalt thou hear in the morning, O LORD; in the morning will I direct my prayer unto thee, and will look up.

How can you stand firm?

1. By Remembering

Psalm 77:10-11
And I said, This is my infirmity: but I will remember the years of the right hand of the most High. 77:11 I will

remember the works of the LORD: surely I will remember thy wonders of old.

The best way for you to be sure of what God wants to do in your life is to remember what He has done in the past.

Verse 10 is a response to the six questions asked in 7-9.

1) Will the Lord reject forever?
2) Will he never show his favor again?
3) Has his unfailing love vanished forever?
4) Has his promise failed for all time?
5) Has God forgotten to be merciful and gracious?
6) Has he in anger withheld his compassion and mercy?

As David remembered those things, suddenly the light of understanding comes on in verse ten and David says "I will remember."

The answer to the doubt that is gathering in his mind is to remember the things the Lord has done. Are you wondering where God is in your time of financial need?

Deuteronomy 8:18
But thou shalt remember the LORD thy God: for it is he that giveth thee power to get wealth, that he may establish his covenant which he sware unto thy fathers, as it is this day.

Are you still waiting for your healing?

Malachi 4:2
But unto you that fear my name shall the Sun of righteousness arise with healing in his wings; and ye shall

go forth, and grow up as calves of the stall.

The key to receiving is to remember:

1) what God has done in the past for you…

Psalm 77:11
I will remember the works of the LORD: surely I will
remember thy wonders of old

These words are given for your encouragement just like a
testimony given by someone who has received a miracle…

2) what He says in His word about the past… Paul wrote
to Timothy in 2 Timothy 2:8-9,

2nd Timothy 2:8-9
…. according to my gospel: 2:9 Wherein I suffer trouble,
as an evil doer, even unto bonds; but the word of God is
not bound.

God's word will be accomplished for those who believe…

3) what He confirms in your spirit about the past and the
present.

According to 1 Corinthians 2:10 God is still revealing
Himself to us by His Spirit.

1st Corinthians 2:10
But God hath revealed them unto us by his Spirit: for the
Spirit searcheth all things, yea, the deep things of God.

When you sense that confirmation in your spirit as to what God wants to do, you can be assured that something good is about to happen. But, your enemy the devil will come against you to tell you that miracles do not happen, what has happened in the past really was not a miracle, and that you are foolish to think that God cares enough about you to do anything in your life.

Peter tells us:

1st Peter 5:8-9
Be sober, be vigilant; because your adversary the devil, as a roaring lion, walketh about, seeking whom he may devour: 5:9 Whom resist stedfast in the faith, knowing that the same afflictions are accomplished in your brethren that are in the world.

Obviously, according to what David has written thus far, the key is remembering. He made a conscious decision to remember the mighty works of God and then to stand firm in them.

How can we stand firm?

2. By Reflecting

Psalm 77:12
I will meditate also of all thy work, and talk of thy doings.

The word meditate in the original language means to murmur or mutter words to yourself. Meditation involves talking things over with yourself to understand what those things mean to you. Meditation means weighing your options. We can look at what God has said in His Word and the miracles we have experienced in the past and then consider what implications those things have on our lives today. What happens inside you when you meditate on God's words and His promises?

Joshua 1:8
This book of the law shall not depart out of thy mouth; but thou shalt meditate therein day and night, that thou mayest observe to do according to all that is written therein: for then thou shalt make thy way prosperous, and then thou shalt have good success.

My father is a carpenter by trade. As I have said he has built many houses. He has designed blueprints for other houses as well as houses he has built. Some houses my father built were from another architects plans. In order to have a well-built house you have to follow the blueprint given, otherwise, the house will fall and not hold up in times of storms or troubles. Dear friend, we have a great architect that drew up the plans for our life. The plan is found in his Word. God has given us the key to having good success and a prosperous way. It is so simple. Study the plan and follow the plan.

Psalm 77:12
I will meditate also of all thy work, and talk of thy doings.

What do God's previous works have to do with your life now? That is something that you need to stop and consider.

How does the fact that God healed throughout the Bible affect us today?

What does it mean to us that God made the sun go backward, the sun stand still, the rain cease for three and a half years and then begin again when Elijah prayed?

What relationship to your life does His word have when it says, "in the last days I will pour out my Spirit on all flesh" or, "And these signs will accompany those who believe: In my name they will drive out demons; they will speak in new tongues… they will place their hands on sick people, and they will get well."

How about when God says if anyone says to this mountain, 'Go, throw yourself into the sea,' and does not doubt in his heart but believes that what he says will happen, it will be done for him.

Are these just idle words from the past that have no meaning today?

These are the words of the Great I AM not the Great I WAS or the Great I MIGHT BE.

I AM forever in the past and the future.
I AM the Alpha and the Omega.
I AM the beginning and the end.
I Am what I have been in the past and will always be in the future.

Hebrews 1:10-12
And, Thou, Lord, in the beginning hast laid the foundation of the earth; and the heavens are the works of thine hands: 1:11 They shall perish; but thou remainest; and they all shall wax old as doth a garment; 1:12 And as a vesture

shalt thou fold them up, and they shall be changed: but thou art the same, and thy years shall not fail.

If God worked miracles in the past He is still willing to do it today. Reflect on God's word and you will see His nature.

How can we stand firm?
By remembering.
By reflecting. And finally:

3. By Responding

Psalm 77:13-15
Thy way, O God, is in the sanctuary: who is so great a God as our God? 77:14 Thou art the God that doest wonders: thou hast declared thy strength among the people. 77:15 Thou hast with thine arm redeemed thy people, the sons of Jacob and Joseph.

Joshua says we are to meditate on the "Book of the Law" day and night. Study it until you know it well. But he does not stop there. Once you have studied it put it into practice.

Joshua 1:8
... thou mayest observe to do according to all that is written therein: for then thou shalt make thy way prosperous, and then thou shalt have good success.

Why do we remember God's miracles?
Why do we reflect or meditate on God's word?
It is not so we can glory in the past, but so we can live in expectation of the future.

It is so that we can know who we are and what we have as God's people.

Psalm 77:14-15
77:14 Thou art the God that doest wonders: thou hast declared thy strength among the people. 77:15 Thou hast with thine arm redeemed thy people,....

1) He is holy. If our God were not a holy God then what need would we have for salvation? We could then be good enough by our own efforts to attain heaven. What response should we have to that?

1 Peter 1:16
Because it is written, Be ye holy; for I am holy.

We have the ability to live holy lives. Because He is holy, we can be holy.

2) He performs miracles.

Hebrews 2:3-4
For if the word spoken by angels was stedfast, and every transgression and disobedience received a just recompence of reward; 2:3 How shall we escape, if we neglect so great salvation; which at the first began to be spoken by the Lord, and was confirmed unto us by them that heard him;

Jesus has told us that we would do the same things that He had done and even greater things.

John 14:12
Verily, verily, I say unto you, He that believeth on me, the works that I do shall he do also; and greater works than these shall he do; because I go unto my Father.

We have been told that we can do the greater things. If we have repented of our sins, been baptized in Jesus' name for the remission of our sin and received the Holy Ghost, then, friend, you have the power. All you need is the faith to activate it. How is faith attained?

Romans 10:17
So then faith cometh by hearing, and hearing by the word of God.

3) He displays His power.

Romans 15:18-19
For I will not dare to speak of any of those things which Christ hath not wrought by me, to make the Gentiles obedient, by word and deed, 15:19 Through mighty signs and wonders, by the power of the Spirit of God...

2 Timothy 1:7
For God hath not given us the spirit of fear; but of power, and of love, and of a sound mind.

Because He has given us access through the Holy Spirit to this power, we should be a demonstration of that power.

Matthew 5:14-16
Ye are the light of the world. A city that is set on an hill cannot be hid. 5:15 Neither do men light a candle, and put it under a bushel, but on a candlestick; and it giveth light

*unto all that are in the house. 5:16 Let your light so shine
before men, that they may see your good works, and
glorify your Father which is in heaven.*

4) He redeems His people.

Acts 2:37-39
*Now when they heard this, they were pricked in their
heart, and said unto Peter and to the rest of the apostles,
Men and brethren, what shall we do? 2:38 Then Peter
said unto them, Repent, and be baptized every one of you
in the name of Jesus Christ for the remission of sins, and
ye shall receive the gift of the Holy Ghost. 2:39 For the
promise is unto you, and to your children, and to all that
are afar off, even as many as the LORD our God shall call.*

It is fitting that we finish up with the idea of redemption.
The redemption of mankind, the payment for our sin, is
easy for us to accept. We understand our need for a Savior.
We repent of our sin and ask Jesus to be the Lord of our
lives, are baptized in the name of Jesus for the remission of
our sins. If you have the faith to be saved then you also
have the faith to receive God's miracle in your life.

Now that you have come to the end of this book what has
it done for you?

Many of you, I am sure, will receive your miracle.
Some of you still have doubt.
And others are still trying to figure it all out.

For the last eight chapters of this book, I have been trying
to take you, step-by-step, through the same process that

Joshua and the nation of Israel went through in order to receive the promise God had given.

The last step is to stand firm in your faith in God and His word. Do not let the enemy of your soul dissuade you. He cannot take your promise from you but he will try to get you to hand it over to him. So it is up to you.

What are you going to do?

The answer is to stand firm in the word of God, in the power of God, to receive the miracles of God and all of the promises of God.

I want to take you to a scripture that is not an end but is both a beginning and an end.

Ephesians 6:10-14
Finally, my brethren, be strong in the Lord, and in the power of his might. 6:11 Put on the whole armour of God, that ye may be able to stand against the wiles of the devil. 6:12 For we wrestle not against flesh and blood, but against principalities, against powers, against the rulers of the darkness of this world, against spiritual wickedness in high places. 6:13 Wherefore take unto you the whole armour of God, that ye may be able to withstand in the evil day, and having done all, to stand. 6:14 Stand therefore, having your loins girt about with truth, and having on the breastplate of righteousness;

Friend, if God's Holy, written Word is true, which it is, get in it, claim every promise and stand firm.

Your miracle is waiting on you today.